FAITH IN SPITE OF ALL—
A Rabbi's Story

FAITH IN SPITE OF ALL—
A RABBI'S STORY

RABBI JUDA GLASNER

VANTAGE PRESS

NEW YORK   WASHINGTON   ATLANTA   HOLLYWOOD

FIRST EDITION

*All rights reserved, including the right
of reproduction in whole or in part in any form.*

Copyright © 1974 by Rabbi Juda Glasner

Published by Vantage Press, Inc.
516 West 34th Street, New York, New York 10001

Manufactured in the United States of America

Standard Book Number 533-01568-5

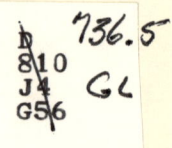

ACKNOWLEDGMENTS

The author gratefully acknowledges the encouragement he received from:

    Rabbi Miklos Hauer
    Solomon Frankel
    Bernard Spiegel

in the writing of this book. He also wishes to express his gratitude to:

    Americanism Educational League
    David Berger
    Sidney Chambers
    Christians and Jews For Law and Morality

Stanley Diller	Ted Orden
George Gluck	Romy and Flora Rosman
Ernest Hancz	Maxine Waltz Ross
Sol Kest	Blanca Roven
Louis Kesten	Herman Schwartz
Flossy Landow	David and Fela Shapell
Alex Lichtig	Joe Simon
Al Loevinger	Aron Spiegel
Armin Mandel	Dan Srulovics
Sam Menlo	Ray Swidler
Marion Miller	Tov Tobias
Eugene Nasch	E. Wintner
Julius Nasch	Gary Wintner

    They all share my belief that this book will contribute to the understanding of our gravest problem, namely the crisis of Faith in our time.

    May the Almighty bestow His blessing on them for their noble deeds.

CONTENTS

Preface	
Foreword	xi
Satan Leads the Dance	1
A People of Scapegoats . . . Separation from my Family	11
Internment and Departure for Poland	23
Escape from Slavery	31
Jewish Lives—Merchandise for Barter	47
Bucharest—I Receive a Diplomatic Passport	59
Interlude in Budapest	75
Switzerland and Sweden	93
America, Land of Freedom . . . A Nation Under God	107
The Invincible Weapon of Faith	125
No Involvement	139
Below the Surface—Beyond the Horizon: Détente or Subterfuge?	157

APPENDIXES

Appendix I. The Jewish Councils—A Cruel Invention	173
Appendix II. A Short History of Hungarian Anti-Semitism—The Accusation of Ritual Murder of Tisza Eszlár	183
Index	197

PREFACE

The historic content of this book would alone be sufficient to merit the attention and interest of any person, young or old, who feels troubled by the deplorable conditions of tension and tumult which bear upon all peoples of the world today. However, beyond its historic significance you will find in this work an inspiring example of courage and perseverance as you follow the author through the torturous trials and tribulations he suffered in his determination to find and re-unite himself with his family from whom he, as had millions of others, been forcibly separated by the Nazis during the horrendous times of Hitler's reign. You will wonder how one man . . . alone could endure such mental and physical torture and survive, not only to pursue his own purpose, but to find ways by which he could render aid to untold numbers of others.

This is the story of Rabbi Juda Glasner, and as you read, you will come to understand whence came the courage and strength to survive. It came from the author's unwavering faith in God, to whom he has devoted his life in faithful servitude.

I have never known a man of such rare human qualities as are demonstrated by Rabbi Juda Glasner. I am proud and grateful and spiritually uplifted to have him as my friend.

HARRY VON ZELL
March 27, 1974

FOREWORD

Neither shalt thou stand idly by the blood of thy fellow-men:
I am the Lord—Leviticus 19:16.

The author of this book, survivor of both the Nazi and the Communist oppression, has increasingly felt that he had to tell the story of how the above command has not been heeded or what has not happened which could have prevented the terrible castastrophe of the extermination of millions of Jews. Sustained by his unshakeable faith in God in times of the greatest test of human will, he wishes to bear testimony to the acts of omission which permitted Hitler to carry out his devilish plans in Europe. He has been an eyewitness to the tragedy of the Jews in Hungary, and the book will address itself especially to this chapter of the immensely sad history of World War II.

The occupation of Hungary by Nazi Germany occurred in March, 1944. At that time the final defeat of the Hitlerian hordes had become a foregone conclusion. In spite of, or perhaps because of this fact, the occupiers, aided by the too willing Hungarian authorities, carried out their plan for extermination of the Jewish population of Hungary with systematic cruelty. Pressed by time, they acted with greater brutality and in greater haste than in any other territory temporarily under Hitler's thumb.

A review of the events that took place at that time will show that there were opportunities which, had they been seized by those in a position to help, could have allowed for the rescue of a large number or maybe all of the unfortunate victims of the Nazis in Hungary. Today we know whatever was done in that direction was too little and came too late.

The German Pastor Niemoeller, who will always be remembered for his courageous stand against Hitler, summarized the stand-off attitude of the outside world which caused the Hungarian tragedy in this statement: "When Communists were jailed, I was not a Communist. When Jews were jailed, I was not a Jew. When union members were jailed, I was not a union member, and when Catholics were jailed, I was not a Catholic. But when I was jailed, it was too late to do anything about it." His statement repeats the old maxim that whoever remains indifferent to the loss of freedom by anyone, risks the forfeiture of his own freedom, and ultimately is bound to pay very dearly for his apathy. George Bernard Shaw said the same thing in other words: "The worst sin toward our fellow creatures is not to hate them, but to be indifferent to them."

The author's personal story integrates into the great collective tragedy of the time. The Nazi danger has now passed, but to tell the truth without bias and without fear, is never without danger. To illustrate this let me refer to the testimony of the Rev. Richard Wurmbrand, a crusader for religious revival in the countries of official atheism and a refugee from Communist prisons, made before a United States Senate Committee. Before leaving Rumania, the Communists told him: "You now are leaving this country but be careful of how you behave abroad. You may preach Christianity, but beware of attacking us. If you speak against Communism, bear in mind that for a mere one thousand dollars it is easy to find someone ready to liquidate you. We are playing with our cards on the table. Remember, in prison you met people we had brought back even from the West."

The faith that sustained me in past tribulations prompts me to proclaim the urgent need for a restoration of the belief in a Divine Being. Only such a belief will give us the moral strength to withstand the otherwise unbearable pressure of our frantic times. This needs to be proclaimed because, unfortunately, millions have lost this belief or never had it; without it they are drifting in a world without directions and without apparent aim, unable ever to quench their thirst for meaning. It is like the story of a lady who reprimanded her servant for leaving dust on the furniture. The servant retorted, "If you will kindly wipe your eyeglasses you will see that there is not a speck of dust anywhere."

Those who do not see the beauty and the glory of faith look at the world through grimy glasses that make everything appear dim to them.

It is my ardent wish that this book will help readers to rekindle the sparks of their faith. However, I do not want to sound like the girl who declared to her mother that she was going to draw a picture of God.

"No one knows what God looks like," the mother objected.

The child replied, "They will after I have finished my picture."

FAITH IN SPITE OF ALL—

A Rabbi's Story

SATAN LEADS THE DANCE

> Oh, that my head were waters, and my eyes a fountain of tears; and that I might weep day and night, for the fallen of my people!—Jeremiah 8:23.

I did not suspect in my youth that one day a story would be building up in my soul and that I would feel compelled to communicate it to my fellow-men. Happy people, they used to say, have nothing to relate about themselves, for happiness is not an event but a state, a condition, undisturbed as long as it lasts. My adolescence and early manhood were such uninterrupted bliss. Descendant of an ancient family of rabbis, I was simply to step into the shoes of my ancestors, to preach the word, a latter-day heir to those who received the commands from God and transmitted them to their flocks. I studied theology in Bratislava, Czechoslovakia, and then again in Montreux, Switzerland. At the age of twenty-two I was a fully ordained Rabbi, a Deputy to my father, the Chief Rabbi of our community of Cluj (the Hungarian Kolozsvár), capital of Transylvania. This was a territory situated in the easternmost part of Hungary, bordering Rumania. Our city had a large and alert Jewish population, and our congregation of some four thousand families was composed of a majority of intelligent and educated people who managed to continue their religious traditions and to keep up with the world at the same time. I married a beautiful girl, also a descendant of rabbis, who was introduced to me in Budapest, after the reattachment of our region to Hungary. Our future seemed to be all cut out for us—continue our dynasty, lead the congregation, partake of the nectar of the Divine Word, by daily studies and daily prayers; a most enviable destiny. Alas, the Garden of Eden is not to remain the permanent dwelling place of man. Satan sees to it that he be expelled from it; to know a life of hardship and suffering.

In 1941, I was twenty-three years old, but the relatively carefree, easy period of my life ended abruptly. Satan, incarnate in Adolf Hitler, led the dance on the continent of Europe. Since the fall of France, no power was left there to resist his rapacious appetite for conquest. This man, a knight of the slums, a failure as an artist, had become the arbiter of nations. The province of Transylvania where we lived was an apple of discord between Rumania and Hungary, just as Alsace-Lorraine was between France and Germany. Prior to World War I, for a thousand years, it belonged to Hungary, but the population of the territory was racially altered because of the greater birth rate of the Rumanians. Our city remained largely Hungarian in language and culture, but the rural areas were in the majority inhabited by Rumanians. The latter did not enjoy under their Hungarian masters the rights that a democratic state ordinarily grants to national minorities. Rumanians had few schools of their own on the elementary or secondary level and there were no Rumanian universities in Hungary. There were no books or newspapers published in that language, and the courts of Transylvania interpreted the law in Hungarian alone. Rumanian intellectuals had to study at Hungarian universities or go to Rumania proper to get a higher education.

The same attitude prevailed in Hungary toward other minorities, Slovaks, Croats and Germans, which explains why these minorities aspired to be united to the countries of their ethnic origin. As a result, Hungary, one of the losers in World War I, saw its territory severely mangled by the Versailles Treaty. Transylvania became part of Rumania, and the former masters became themselves a national minority.

Hitler needed both Hungary and Rumania to secure the flanks of Germany to get supplies and food for his armies. The question of Transylvania was submitted to his arbitration. The fact that he made his decision and that it was obeyed without any intervention or protest by a single nation in Europe demonstrated his absolute power at the time. Europe lay prostrate at his feet. England, the only country that was still opposing him, was too preoccupied with her own survival to play any role in the matter.

Hitler settled the conflict about Transylvania by a Solomon's verdict, adjudging one-half of it, including the city of Cluj, to Hungary, leaving the other half to Rumania. This verdict did not satisfy either of the parties, but it was carried out just the same. Our Cluj retrieved its former name of Kolozsvár, and the Hungarian upper-middle class received the entering Hungarian troops with jubilation.

Never shall I forget that night of the 17th of September, 1940. The intoxicated soldiery was not to be held back, nor was there any will on the part of their officers to do so. On the contrary, Rumanians and Jews became the free prey of these savages, at least in the night of their entry in the city and the first few days that followed it. They looted and raped and massacred their victims wholesale. It was the first time that I witnessed what is called lawlessness: the weak finding no protection from the violence of the strong; the life of the jungle succeeding civilization without any warning: man becoming a menace to man; a whole city, made beautiful by the labor of generations, turning into a scene of wanton destruction; drunken devils breaking into houses, taking what they wanted, beating innocent people, blood, curses, tears, screams, accompanying their steps. War has its laws; the unleashing of human beasts upon a helpless population has none. The fury of these bandits was incomprehensible to us. After all, what had Cluj or

Kolozsvár done to them? to Hungary? After the attribution of Transylvania to Rumania by the Versailles Treaty in 1918, cultural life, both Rumanian and Hungarian, developed there rapidly. The Rumanian university in Cluj prided itself upon its Medical School, reputed the best in Southeast Europe. Medical scholars of international reputation were attracted to its faculty; students flocked there from many countries; patients came for diagnosis and cure.

The city of Cluj breathed a cultural atmosphere that was exceedingly stimulating. The Hungarians continued to publish their books and newspapers, had their schools in their own language from the elementary to university level. They attended their own theaters, argued their lawsuits in their mother tongue as though there had been no change in the government. The Jewish community possessed in Cluj a theological seminary, seat of scholarship and learning. It is an irony of history that the daily Jewish newspaper, *Ujkelet,* was published in Hungarian, a proof of the fact that most of the Jews felt at ease in that language. This paper was suspended immediately after the reoccupation of the city by Hungary. In spite of enjoying these democratic freedoms, the Hungarians could not forgive the fact that the Rumanians, whom they considered inferior, had become the ruling nation in the state. They would not accept the new situation. Almost from the first day of the change-over they pursued an active irredentist propaganda campaign both inside Hungary and abroad. Their slogan had been, *"Nem, nem, soha!"* (No, no, never!); they were poisoned, as it were, by the passion of their own words. Now, thanks to Hitler, they had an opportunity to vent their pent-up frustrations. In their own bestial way they proved to themselves and to the world that they had once more become the masters. . . .

For me and my family, the change in the local government represented a personal disaster. Indeed, we grew attached to the Rumanians who were more broadminded, more pleasant in their personal relations than were the often proud and conceited Hungarians. For a few days, the Jews of Kolozsvár did not dare to show themselves on the streets. A friend of my father's, a Jew who nevertheless was an ardent Hungarian patriot, who resided in the part of Transylvania that remained Rumanian after Hitler's arbitration, hearing about the reattachment of our city to Hungary, had left his family and came to salute the Hungarian flag and the troops that carried it. He was murdered the night of his arrival.

The events of those first days of the Hungarian occupation of our city constituted a shock for me. I realized that with Hitler playing the patron of the Hungarian nation, we Jews must expect great hardships to come upon us. The authorities of the state would undoubtedly introduce new anti-semitic laws, harsher than any of the past. Perhaps the infamous Nuremberg edicts that reduced the German Jews to pariahs as early as 1935, four years before the outbreak of World War II, would be imitated by the Hungarian authorities who were body and soul devoted to Hitler.

Through Jonel Pop, former Chief of Police under the Rumanians, we were for the time being informed of any measures concerning Jews contemplated by the new regime. Though he was no longer in office, he maintained good relations with the Hungarian authorities. He spoke both Rumanian and Hungarian, and his influence was invaluable. Through Pop we also received news coming from Budapest, seat of the Hungarian government.

Mr. Pop assured me that he would facilitate our passing to Rumanian territory whenever our lives were in danger. We gratefully thanked him for this offer and mentally kept it in abeyance; yet when the time came to avail ourselves of it, moral considerations—as I shall relate it—prevented us from taking advantage of this opportunity.

The year 1941 represented the peak of Hitler's power. As time went on, the superiority in manpower and raw materials of the Western allies made itself felt more and more. Hungary, dragged into the war on the side of

Germany, suffered grievous losses along with the latter.

Entire Hungarian divisions were annihilated in Russia. The Hungarian army was insufficiently trained and equipped for modern warfare, and the economy of the country was too shaky to sustain the strain. There was general discontent in the land. Rumors circulated to the effect that Regent Horthy was seeking to enter into negotiations with the Allies with a view to concluding a separate peace with them. The rumors expressed the general wish of the nation and certainly that of every clear-thinking person. Indeed, by the beginning of the year 1944 it became obvious to every observer that Hitler had lost the war.

The change in the political atmosphere in Hungary did not escape the attention of the Germans. They had reason to fear Hungary's defection. It threatened to entail the breaking-up of the entire hinterland of the German armies. The vast territories they controlled threatened to rise and turn into a domestic front of enemies.

To ward off this danger, Hitler decided to change the status of Hungary from a friendly to an occupied country on March 19, 1944. He resorted to the same strategy that had worked in Czechoslovakia. He invited Regent Horthy to visit him at his headquarters in Germany, in order to discuss important problems interesting both their countries. He entertained his guest, started sham discussions with him, while his troops were put on the alert ready to cross the borders of Hungary. As soon as the preparations were finished, he presented the Regent with the brutal fact and demanded that he sign an address to the Hungarian nation to welcome the German troops as friends and protectors of the country. Horthy's protest was brushed aside; he would not be permitted to return to Hungary unless he complied with Hitler's ultimatum. When he did return, he found his residence, the former royal castle of Budapest, surrounded by German guards. Horthy and the nation became hostages and prisoners of Hitler.

The forces committed to the occupation of Hungary

were small. The Germans relied on the cooperation of high-ranking Hungarian officers, known for their Nazi sympathies. They were to see to it that no resistance should be offered to the occupiers. Only in places where the orders of these traitors arrived late or were not transmitted, did the Germans meet with any opposition.

We, in Kolozsvár, did not receive the doubtful blessing of their entry immediately. Only the newspapers changed overnight; their tone became wildly enthusiastic in their praise of Germany. Even those among them which in the past had been rather lukewarm or frankly hostile to the German alliance outdid each other to protest their friendship and affection for "the great neighbor, protector of the small."

For me, this change of tone of the newspapers was more of an eye-opener than anything else I had witnessed before. It offered me an insight into the dark side of human nature. Was it possible, I asked myself, that people foreswear so easily principles by which they had lived and which they preached at the slightest pressure put upon them? Where was the sanctity of the written word? Where were faith and sincerity of beliefs?

I asked myself these questions because I was young, and dedicated to my calling as a spiritual leader. I felt that betraying one's beliefs is the worst betrayal, because it meant the abdication of human dignity. Such self-debasement provoked contempt by others; it would be punished— I obscurely recognized—by calculated debasement on the part of the masters of the day. Subsequent events justified my subconscious or semi-conscious fears. What I did not know then was that the Nazis based their plans of world domination exactly on this premise of self-debasement on the part of their defeated enemies.

The newspapers of Budapest narrated the events that occurred in the capital since the German occupation. The take-over had obviously been planned and prepared both in Germany and in Hungary itself. During the night and the day following the occupation of the country, vehicles carrying troops of the SS, armed with machine guns, ran back and forth through the streets. Their aim was to arrest all known or potential enemies of Germany and to secure the occupation. The SS officers were provided with blacklists by their Hungarian accomplices. Politicians, members of Parliament or of the Upper House, aristocrats, diplomats, journalists, attorneys, anyone known to be hostile to the German brand of national-socialism, even the head of the Hungarian counter-intelligence and his assistant, were taken into custody. The Social-Democratic Party, a well-organized political unit, found itself without leaders all at once; they were all captured on that first day of German invasion.

Among the prisoners of the new masters were Keresztes-Fischer, Minister of the Interior and his principal collaborators. Keresztes-Fischer had held his office for more than ten years. He constituted the greatest thorn in the side of the Hungarian Nazis and of their German friends, for he stood firmly for law and the rights of the individual. He professed his faith in democracy and in the parliamentary system which made him the much-hated target of all political adventurers. In spite of enormous pressures exerted on Hungarian leaders since the advent of Hitler, he had succeeded in making the life of the Jewish citizens in Hungary the most tolerable in the entire area subject to German domination.

Within thirty-six hours, Hungarian political life was swept clean of all the people who in the past had shown the courage of standing up for their convictions, and who could have, because of their prestige, made the nazification of Hungary difficult for the invaders. Most of these men were deported to Germany under the most brutal conditions. Only a few were kept in Hungarian prisons.

They were the first line of victims. They were followed by lesser personalities, secretaries, employees of liberal organizations, writers, anyone who in the past decade had at any time spoken out or shown hostility to Germany.

Obviously the Germans possessed detailed files on everyone in the public view.

The government, of uncertain loyalty, was dismissed, and a new one, composed of Hitler's Hungarian supporters, was formed. It took four days to set up such a government. Indeed, responsible politicians were reluctant to cooperate; moreover, the Regent himself was reported to be unwilling to sanction the change brought about by force. At last, however, the Nazis succeeded in filling the cabinet posts under the leadership of a certain Döme Sztojay, an unknown until that time.

I can assert without hesitation that not only us Jews, but most of the Gentiles I knew, indeed the immense majorit of the members of the middle class in our city were shocked and dismayed by the turn of events. They all realized that the presence of the Germans in our country foreboded a new, perhaps irreparable catastrophe. As to the Jewish population, they, just as I and my family, feared the worst. From morning till late evening, our house was filled with people anxious to talk to us, their leaders, hoping to get some useful advice, some encouragement, to find a ray of hope through our words. What could we tell them? Speak against our conviction; declare that after all the future might not be as gloomy as they feared; that Hungary was not Germany, and pious statements of a similar nature. Nevertheless, we advised them that whoever had the means of leaving, of passing to Rumanian territory, should do so. I spoke to Mr. Pop about that, and he promised that he would intervene with the border guards, so that they should not be too strict with permits to cross over. He urged us to leave as soon as possible, but we replied that we had to put off this decision till later, because our duty required us to remain with our congregation. Actually, we greatly hesitated to face this problem. My father, especially, was firmly opposed to our departure.

The crisis in our lives mirrored the crisis in the outside world. It forced me to rely upon my inner resources in facing it. My past appeared to me suddenly as unreal, or rather, the present took up an aspect of total unreality in relationship to my past. I had lived in contact with God; lofty thoughts had separated me from the fight and ugliness of the everyday world. Now this everyday world was invading my inner world, trying to impress me as the only reality. A terrible feeling of loneliness and helplessness assailed me at times, and also doubts as to the effectiveness of the preaching of God's word in influencing man's orientation. Fortunately, I succeeded in shaking off this feeling of despair. The arguments I brought forth in my solitary meditations, in the debate over the reality of Hitler versus the reality of God, ended with the conviction firmer than ever that Hitler carried with him the seeds of his own destruction, that the victory of Satan was, by its very essence, the prelude to his eventual downfall. This conviction did, however, not blind me as to the possibility of terrible tragedies among my friends and in our own immediate future. I said to myself that I had to await with firmness whatever fate had in store for me. "This is the criterion of my faith:" I said to myself, "whether it will sustain me enough to make me remain a believer in my own higher destiny, whether it will give me courage to endure hardships, suffering, even death."

The very suddenness of the crisis around me and within me sharpened my insight. I felt pain and joy at the same time: pain at parting with my carefree past, joy in knowing that I was trying to gain inner strength from chaos, despair and fear. I learned that true victory of the individual can only be gained by facing himself in solitary confrontation.

Many things happened to me and to the world in the months and years that followed, but that first debate with myself in those days of obvious, imminent danger constituted for me an unparalleled reward, that of stepping higher on the ladder toward self-confidence and self-esteem, and especially toward the confidence in, and the love of, God.

A PEOPLE OF SCAPEGOATS ...
SEPARATION FROM MY FAMILY

We Hungarian Jews had good reasons to fear the worst after the constitution of the Sztojay government. We realized that the German occupation would furnish it the excuse to vent the anti-Jewish feelings long prevalent among landed proprietors, frustrated intellectuals, mediocrities of all sorts. In fact, anti-semitism as governmental policy originated in Europe in Hungary. Already in the 1880's there arose in the Hungarian parliament a party, the only program of which was the propagation of hatred against the Jews. Its prophet was a certain Gyula Verhovay, a worthy predecessor of Hitler. He founded newspapers, clubs and fraternities, sent out speakers to the four corners of the country spreading the doctrine that the Jews were an alien body in the nation, with ideals pernicious to the moral health of the Hungarians. Verhovay's influence was widespread among the people and did not cease even after the death of the leader and the dissolution of his party.

After the First World War a new anti-semitic movement, called the "Awakening Hungarians," was formed from among disgruntled elements of the lower-middle-classes, from noncommissioned officers, suddenly discharged and jobless, from small clerks with a sprinkling of a few officers. This movement was later taken over by politicians close to Nicholas Horthy, the future Regent of Hungary.

World War I saw the collapse of the Austro-Hungarian

monarchy and the proclamation of the Hungarian Republic under Count Michael Károlyi in 1918. The President of the Republic was a well-meaning, liberal, but weak politician, incapable of bearing the pressure of the times. With the dissolution of the fronts, the disorderly retreat of the armies, and especially as a result of the occupation of Hungarian territories by Rumanian, Czech and Yugoslav troops, he threw in the sponge and handed over the reins of government to the Communists. Among these the strong man was Béla Kun, Moscow-trained, a personal friend of Lenins. He was Jewish and so were two or three other members of his regime. This fact was sufficient for many to equate Communism with the Jews and to declare that the Jews were out to rule the world and that they were the enemies of mankind. Hungary subsequently introduced several anti-Jewish laws of increasing severity. Only 6% of Jewish students were to be admitted to Hungarian universities; those admitted had to sit in the last benches of classrooms, called "benches of shame." They were often beaten up by their fellow students without any protection on the part of the University authorities.

In fact, under Regent Horthy, Hungary became the forerunner of Jewish persecution as a means of political propaganda, and as a governmental policy. To a degree the racist policy adopted by Horthy and his successive governments contributed to a new era of political backwardness in Europe, a policy that had been banned from the continent since the end of the 19th century.

The Sztojay government, composed of men devoted body and soul to Hitler, considered its first and foremost task to issue a number of anti-Jewish ordinances. They followed each other in rapid succession, like bullets shot from a machine gun. It became obvious to any observer that the plan of gradual annihilation of the Hungarian Jews had been drawn up prior to the occupation and was handed down to straw men put into position by the occupiers.

The edicts of the new government were posted on the

walls of our city. Everywhere crowds gathered to read them. Some of them commented on them, mostly in shocked and disapproving terms. There were however, people who showed a certain malicious joy upon reading what amounted to the virtual enslavement of their Jewish fellow citizens.

The principal of these measures were:

1. Jews were forbidden to leave the limits of the localities in which they resided.
2. They were forbidden to use trains, ships, hired cars, bicycles, the front part of street cars. They had to turn in all vehicles in their possession.
3. Jews were not allowed to listen to the radio. All radio sets in their possession had to be delivered to the authorities.
4. They were immediately deprived of the privilege of subscribing to telephones.
5. They were compelled to wear conspicuously, in a manner that it could not be easily removed, the yellow Star of David, for the purpose of easy recognition.
6. Jews could shop in grocery stores or markets only between 11:00 A.M. and 1:00 P.M.; other stores could only be visited between 1:00 and 3:00 P.M.
7. No Jew, no matter what his age, was allowed to hire Aryan domestic personnel.
8. All Jewish commercial enterprises were to be closed forthwith. Jewish assets of any kind—bank accounts, outstanding payments, cash, real estate, gold or jewelry—were confiscated.
9. Jewish attorneys, engineers, journalists, actors, were to be dismissed without notice.
10. All Jewish employees had to be dismissed with the exception of a few who were indispensable for the moment, but those too had to be replaced within four months at the latest.
11. Jewish physicians were not allowed to treat Aryan

patients. They had to add the Jewish star to their sign so as to make it recognizable that they were Jewish.

12. All books of Jewish authors were withdrawn from libraries, bookstores and publishing houses. They were handed over to the newly founded Institute for Research on Jews for selection for purposes of propaganda. Those not used were reduced to pulp.
13. Jews were issued special food cards which deprived them of eggs, butter, milk, fats of any sort as well as of margarine. They were not allowed to purchase any meat, nor paprika and other condiments. Their rations of sugar, oil, etc., were reduced.
14. Jews were not allowed to buy tobacco.
15. Parallel with these cruel edicts went the concentration of the Jews in ghettos. It began in the provinces where they were herded together in certain parts of the various towns, sealed off from the rest of the population. In the capital, Jews were brought into the so-called Jewish Houses scattered in various districts. These were made conspicuous by an enormous yellow star.
16. All Jewish men between 18 and 28 years of age were summoned to labor service.
17. Jews working in defense establishments, men and women, including the personnel of offices and technicians, were concentrated in barracks.

Never in human history had edicts of such malicious cruelty been issued almost overnight against a segment of the population that had hiterto contributed so much to the economic and cultural life of the nation. And these harsh measures, invented by persons with a sick mind, were implemented with the greatest brutality. The Hungarian authorities did everything possible to cause the victims the maximum amount of suffering and torment.

The Minister of the Interior of the puppet government

headed by Sztojay was Andor Jaross, a man of limitless ambition though lacking any distinguishing qualifications. He saw his opportunity in complete devotion to the ideas of National-Socialism. To please the Germans, he appointed two rabid anti-semites, László Endre and László Baky as Undersecretaries for Jewish Affairs, with complete independence as to measures and decisions concerning their department. László Endre especially obtained unlimited power to decide the lives or death of Jews. His chief characteristics were hatred, stemming from a pronounced inferiority complex, and a complete lack of restraint. Prior to his appointment under Sztojay, he had been a judge and governor of a province. In this latter capacity he had issued special anti-Jewish ordinances considered extreme even by his own employees. His family itself regarded him as a psychopath who had never been able to control his passions and had always disregarded the laws of his country.

The other undersecretary for Jewish affairs, László Baky, was a retired general of the gendarmery and a deputy of the Arrow-Crossist (anti-Jewish—pro-Nazi) party. Anti-semitism was a tradition in his family. Indeed, László Baky was the grandson of a judge who in 1882 played an infamous role in the ritual murder trial of Tisza Eszlár. (That used to be called the Hungarian Dreyfus affair which had, at the time, its repercussion throughout the entire continent.) The older Baky did everything in his power to prove that a young girl, by the name of Esther Solymossi, had been murdered by the Jews in order to mix her blood into the unleavened bread eaten by them at the Jewish Passover. His efforts failed thanks to the efforts of an enlightened lawyer who proved the insanity of the charges, but the trial poisoned the moral atmosphere of the country and it took several decades before the waves of distrust and hatred subsided somewhat in the Hungarian society.[*]

---

[*]See Appendix II.

Immediately upon entering his office, Endre held a series of interviews with members of the pro-Nazi press. These interviews all revolved around the Jewish question. The journalists vied with each other to show their sympathy for Endre and to justify the measures implemented against the Jews. Endre and Baky could act with complete immunity because the other members of the cabinet were all equally anxious to obtain the good graces of the occupants.

The press and the radio echoed the most insane, most vicious charges brought against the Jews. Anything anti-Jewish that could be found in world literature was praised as the works of geniuses. "The Protocols of the Elders of Zion," a creation by Alfred Rosenberg, Hitler's racial philosopher, was dished up for intellectual food to the people. Every day forged articles attributed to British or American newspapers were published to vilify the Jewish people and the Jewish race. Whenever the newspapers singled out one Hungarian Jewish individual, profferring trumped-up charges against him, the individual in question was arrested within the hour after the publication of the newspaper.

Prior to the concentration of the Jews in the ghetto, the former Chief of Police Pop called me.

"All the Jews will be deported shortly! A ghetto has already been established in Kassa," Mr. Pop reported.

He had learned that twelve thousand Jews were massed in the latter city in a brickyard. It was the gendarmery, the rural police, rather than the police of the towns, who were assigned by Endre to carry out the concentration of the Jews in the provinces. Endre obviously knew his men, knew whom to trust to carry out any measures, even the most inhuman ones.

I transmitted this terrifying report through clandestine channels to some key members of our congregation, for we were at that time completely isolated from each other. I advised them to do whatever they could to put their families, their possessions and themselves in safety. Safety was, by that time, an impossibility, for the borders had been sealed off on Endre's orders. Twenty-four hours after Kassa, it was the turn of our own city. The Jews of Kolozsvár were given one hour to get ready to be taken to their place of concentration. Young and old, women and children, all had to go.

I can't ever forget those days. The sky seemed to have collapsed over our heads. The confusion and despair reigning among the intended deportees was extreme. Grabbing at random some of their belongings, dazed, not understanding, people aligned themselves on the streets, immediately flanked by the gendarmes, armed to the teeth, formidable-looking, merciless, threatening devils. They hurried their victims, drove them on, often forbidding them to take some food and something to cover their bodies with. Off the long line of the wretched went, marching toward a brickyard in the outskirts of the city, marching toward their destiny.

For some reason that I cannot explain, the gendarmes, who dragged out most of our coreligionists, ordered us along with a few other families, to stay. "We will come back for you!" one of the gendarmes added, looking us over. I said to myself that perhaps these devils had received instructions to spare us and a handful of other people temporarily. At any rate, the delay had to be only a temporary one. We had no illusions. Our turn would come soon.

Before entering their place of concentration, the Jews were ordered to deposit any money or valuables they might have brought with them, for they would be searched upon entering. Woe to those on whose bodies the guards found anything that could be regarded as valuable. They were beaten to insensibility. The approach to the ghetto was off-limits for the rest of the population so that no food nor anything else could be smuggled in to alleviate the plight of the unfortunates inside.

As the footsteps of the gendarmes were no longer heard, and the crowd of the victims had departed, a terrible silence settled on the streets and upon our souls also. We were no longer afraid of anything; we were beyond fear and despair. We had faced worse than death; the degradation of man.

"What shall we do?" we asked.

"We can still cross the border. Mr. Pop would surely help us, in spite of the strict surveillance," I opined.

"We have no right to save ourselves," my father objected. "If we escape and abandon our people, what will our lives be worth? How would we face ourselves? What kind of leaders do we pretend to be?"

My mother spoke up, "Don't you think that, just because you are leaders of the Jewish people, you have an obligation to save yourselves?"

My wife and my sister seemed to concur in this latter view, but my father remained adamant. "We must share the suffering of our people," he said, "just as we shared their joys. We shall stay, whatever will happen to us."

I looked at my father as he was thus speaking. An emotion that I cannot describe made my heart beat faster, and at the same time sent a chill down my spine. Never had he appeared to me more venerable than at that moment. It seemed to me that God himself had spoken through his words, for there was something infinitely lofty in them. Yet, such is human nature! A voice in me, the voice of self-preservation, protested that to obey him would mean to be irrevocably doomed, and that we all, everyone of us, would perish in the holocaust that was engulfing our coreligionists. Real heroism in the lives of the humans does not necessarily manifest itself in noisy, public actions. It can and very often it does occur in silent moments, lived in private seclusion. I knew that I would accept my father's verdict, and that I would obey him even though every fibre in me protested against it. He was the hero and I felt ashamed before him. At the same time, deep down there was also joy in me—the joy of being my father's son. The word "covenant" upon which I had meditated in former years, all at once stood out with a new meaning and a new splendor in my mind's eye. The word meant bowing to

God's will, accepting it, attempting to rise toward Him through suffering, humiliation, death, whatever fate might have in store for me. I recalled the novels and stories of Dostoevski, my favorite reading outside of the Talmud, and wondered how real, how true the situation and dilemmas of his heroes had become before me through my own situation and my own dilemma.

There was a silence among us. The women looked dejected, dismayed. My wife undoubtedly thought of our little boy; would his young life end abruptly in some horror camp? My mother ventured to say, "If we stay, if we all perish, who would carry on after the storm has passed?"

It occurred to me that perhaps there was some sort of solution.

"I will present myself to do service in a labor camp. There, my life might be safe whatever I may have to bear otherwise. Our lineage will then be preserved, and I may do something for our people, for those who will survive."

Such a solution, in my own eyes, was one of practical and moral compromise. It satisfied the vital instinct in me by the prospect of probable survival. It also appeased my conscience, or so it seemed to me, by telling myself that my survival was in the interest of the Jewish people and of all people, all my brethren to whom I had dedicated my life. All the above flashed through my mind at that moment. Things were not quite clear to me, but such was the essence of my feelings and my thoughts as I am now trying to analyze them.

My resolution to separate from my family and volunteer for labor service was still further justified in my own eyes, because I was fully aware that it would entail tremendous suffering on my part. I am not speaking only of the moral suffering of leaving with the knowledge that my beloved were in the immediate danger of being taken away to face an unknown destination, possibly death, but also of the physical suffering that the notion of labor service then represented to me. Indeed the words "labor service" were a euphemism that concealed the most cruel treatment of those who were subject to it, my fellow Jews. The prevailing principle among the anti-semitic leaders of Hungary was that one could not trust the Jews with weapons. They should, therefore, not be enrolled in regular Army units, but constrained to serve the military effort of the country just the same by doing all the hard work connected with army operations. Under this principle, the Jewish youth enrolled in labor camps were regarded and treated as slaves without any rights, at the mercy of sergeants and officers who commanded them. Many of the latter were psychologically conditioned to look upon human material placed into their power as inferior creatures, harmful to the welfare of mankind, and as criminal elements to be watched and punished, or they were sadists, seizing the opportunity to satisfy their morbid craving for inflicting suffering. In the past few years, we had received lamentable reports to the effect that the inmates of labor camps had been savagely beaten, forced to dig ditches, starved, abused in every way. One report said that in one camp they had been ordered to climb on trees and jump from one tree to another like monkeys, forbidden to utter articulate sounds, and that those who, exhausted, fell from the trees, were beaten with the butts of rifles and finally shot. There were even more horrible reports which one blushes to reproduce.

All this information was known to me, and present in my mind at the moment when I suggested that I would volunteer for labor service. This knowledge gave weight and importance to my proposal. Deep down, in the farthest corner of my subconscious, there was a willingness to offer my expected suffering to God. The Almighty would examine my heart and watch over me. He would not abandon us, his servants, in the hour of our greatest need.

My suggestion was at first received with loud protests. "Don't go, don't leave us alone!" my wife exclaimed. "Whatever will happen to us, it should happen to all of us together!"

My mother concurred. "Think of your wife. Think of your little child. Who will protect them if you are not with us?"

I felt depressed, miserable. What could I use to oppose such words?

Again, my father spoke up last.

"Juda is right," he said. "He can do more for you, for us, by joining the labor service than by waiting here to be deported. Also, he will most likely preserve himself that way. His being there may even protect us in some way. After all, the labor service is under military command; the authorities may consider that he is fulfilling his duty toward the country and spare us from whatever the Germans decide against the Jews."

His reasoning at that time might appear tenuous on the surface in retrospect, but we were in a desperate situation and had very little choice. We had no illusions as to the fate we could expect. And again in retrospect, beyond the narrow limits of common-sense reasoning, my father's wisdom once more proved to be right. My separation from my family would save them and would save me. At the crossroads of our destinies, I had to choose the road that temporarily led me away from them. I had to go my separate way in order to retrieve them later on.

I tried to be strong at the moment when I said "Good bye" to my wife, when I kissed my baby, when I embraced my mother, my father, my younger sister. My strength was the only thing I could give them at the moment of our separation. I caressed my crying wife, and I wiped the tears from my mother's face. I made a great effort not to falter myself.

"We have been the spokesmen of our people before God," I said. "We have been leaders of men. Shall we not show them an example of courage now?"

The women cried. They did not answer. My father said simply, "Leave us, my son; God be with you!" He put his two hands on my head and blessed me.

I left the house of my parents immediately, and hurried to present myself to the military authorities. It was extremely urgent for me to do so, for the return of the gendarmes could be expected momentarily.

In the barracks I pointed out that, as a rabbi, I had been deferred from labor camp, but that I wished to fulfill this obligation. I knew that the officer who looked over my papers was aware of the reason for my action. If he was pro-Nazi, he would not accept me and would hand me over to the gendarmes for deportation. I also knew that the army was not in complete agreement with the higher-ups in the government; it resented being commanded by a foreign, occupying power.

The officer signed my enrollment, and I was in the hands of the military where the gendarmes could not touch me.

"Which one is better," I wondered, "which kind of slavery?"

There we were, my family expecting to be taken to the ghetto, and I myself in the barracks.

"We are back in Egypt, under the Pharaohs," I thought. "Will God lead us out into freedom, as he had done once before with our people?"

I wanted to answer this question in the affirmative, to give myself hope and confidence. I was determined to remain alive.

INTERNMENT AND DEPARTURE FOR POLAND

From the barracks I was sent to Nagybánya, a little town not quite fifty miles north of Cluj, that constituted the assembly place for labor campers. I took with me the image of the two women and of the baby, the image of the old man bent by grief. I carried with me the knowledge that they would be taken to the newly established ghetto, and from there to some unknown destination. I was a speck of dust in a dust storm, stirred by a whirlwind. I was conscious of my helplessness and this feeling weighed upon me. I said to myself, however, that millions were at that time just as helpless as I was, and that all storms abate eventually. That very same feeling of helplessness gave me courage and the determination to endure.

In Nagybánya luck at first accompanied my steps. I was assigned to an officer as his servant. He was an educated man, a teacher in civilian life. When he learned that I was a rabbi, he treated me with consideration, more like a friend than like a servant. I felt grateful to God, for I saw in my lucky situation the proof of His providence.

Through the officer, I learned that my family had been, indeed, interned in the ghetto in Cluj. I entreated him to use his influence so that I would be permitted to enter the ghetto to pay a visit to my beloved. I was terribly upset by reports that many people there, particularly those who were known to have been well-off, were subjected to cruel interrogation accompanied by torture to make them reveal the hiding place of their valuables. I had even heard that my father also had been taken for interrogation. I was almost losing my mind worrying about him. Had he, too, been mistreated, tortured like the others? Later, I learned that he had succeeded in persuading the torturers that he possessed nothing of value. He was allowed to go without anyone laying a hand on him. In this fact I saw a miracle. Out of so many hundreds insulted, beaten, tortured, he was the only one they had left go unharmed.

"They will never let you into the ghetto, or if they do, you would never get out again," the officer explained to me, "but I can take you to Cluj, close enough to the ghetto to see your family from a distance."

He kept his word. I saw my dear ones and they saw me. We could not exchange words, but we exchanged glances, gleams from our eyes that traveled to and fro. There they were, apparently in good health, and safe for the moment. In our plight, in spite of our tragedy, I felt about twenty-five feet away from them, separated by the barbed wire of the ghetto, something akin to happiness. That feeling was of course, mixed with pain and grief, but there was also hope that perhaps, by dint of some miracle, one day we would be reunited in safety.

From the officer, I also learned what happened to the Jews in the rest of the provinces. Their concentration in camps was carried out within a few days. Undersecretary Endre went on a country-wide tour to visit the new ghettos. Upon his return to the capital, he called a press conference. He declared that he had personally supervised the establishment of the Jewish camps in thirty-two cities and was satisfied that it had been done "in a spirit of human kindness and Christian humanity." This statement was prompted by the inquiry made by the papal representative to Hungary and for foreign consumption. The astonishing fact is that the foreign envoys accepted at face value the cynical, shameless lies of this notorious anti-semite. President

Roosevelt sent a warning to the Hungarian government on March 24, 1944, concerning the concentration and probable deportation of the Jews. This statement included the following passages:

> In one of the blackest crimes of all history—begun by the Nazis in the day of peace and multiplied by them a hundred times in time of war—the wholesale systematic murder of the Jews of Europe goes on unabated every hour. . . . That these innocent people, who have already survived a decade of Hitler's fury, should perish on the very eve of triumph over the barbarism which their persecution symbolizes, would be a major tragedy.
> It is therefore fitting that we should again proclaim our determination that none who participate in these acts of savagery shall go unpunished. . . . That warning applies not only to the leaders but also to their functionaries and subordinates in Germany and in the satellite countries. All who knowingly take part in the deportation of Jews to their death in Poland or Norwegians and French to their death in Germany are equally guilty with the executioners. All who share the guilt shall share the punishment.
> Hitler is committing these crimes against humanity in the name of the German people. I ask every German and every man everywhere under Nazi domination, to show the world by his action that in his heart he does not share these insane criminal desires. Let him hide these pursued victims, help them to get over their borders, and do what he can to save them from the Nazi hangman. I ask him also to keep watch, and to record the evidence that will one day be used to convict the guilty.

The forewarning by President Roosevelt should have come years earlier to prevent the evildoers from carrying out their satanic designs in Europe. This admonition was transmitted by every conceivable means, including foreign language broadcasts and in leaflets air-dropped by the millions over occupied Europe. Furthermore, the above mentioned text of President Roosevelt's statement was forwarded to the diplomatic representatives of neutral nations and also carried in their newspapers. The British gave their full support to this statement and were circulating the same. However, the Russian government rejected endorsement of the warning and did not support it. Their attitude constituted a pattern which the Russians followed during the entire period of World War II, and continue to follow to this very day.

Endre and Baky, knowing that the German defeat was near, seemed to race against time in trying to implement the plan of complete annihilation of the Jews of Hungary. They hastily began the deportations of those in the camps. In the Northeast, these deportations started around the 15th of May, 1944. The gendarmes supervising them showed themselves worthy of their masters. Not even the Nazis, in their worst excesses, exhibited so much bestiality toward their victims as did the agents of Endre and Baky. It is a sad commentary along with many others about human civilization, that such things could occur in Europe in the middle of the twentieth century. Women were stripped and raped; sick and pregnant women were thrown into freight cars, treated worse than cattle. In Nyiregyháza the deportees were marched through the street in pouring rain. Children over one year old were forced to march with the others. The laggards were driven on by bullwhips. In Sátoraljaujhely, groups of men refused to enter the freight cars. They were shot on the spot.

It should be noted that the Germans wanted to send out on a daily basis one or two trains consisting of forty-five wagons, and containing about thirty-two hundred people. This pace however, was not rapid enough for Endre. He demanded that six trains a day be moved out with twelve or thirteen thousand people each. He mobilized five thousand gendarmes for this purpose. Thanks to Endre, the destruction of Hungarian Jewry was taking place at an incredible speed. By the 12th of June, three hundred ten thousand people had been deported.

My privileged situation with the humane officer did not last. A few days after our return from Cluj to Nagybánya, I was assigned to a labor camp. Hard labor in the camp was all the more strenuous for me because I had not been used to it. Nevertheless, I decided that I would exert every effort to do whatever would be required of me to the best of my strength and ability. To this resolution I owed my life. Indeed, one day our camp in Nagybánya was visited by high-ranking army officers and officers of the gendarmerie. We were all summoned to an "appeal." The officers took turns in drilling us for hours. Those of us who at any moment showed any slowing down, or any lack of response to their commands, were taken out of the camp and disqualified as workers. They were beaten, insulted as good-for-nothing loafers, and taken by gendarmes to the ghetto to be shipped with other victims from Nagybánya to Auschwitz.

Thank God, I was not among them. The drill-gendarmes and officers did not criticize my performance. I saw in this fact proof that my will to endure was an effective force, provided God would lend me health and strength and that He would remain with me. . . .

I was saved from Auschwitz, but my situation was far from enviable. I too was to go to Poland to work there as a slave laborer. We packed our rags and were marched to the railroad station where cattle cars were awaiting us. On the floor of the cars there was some straw. We were also given some bread and there was water in one barrel. As we filed into the cattle cars, there was no bitterness in my heart, at least as my personal situation was concerned. I remembered what I had heard about the way the unfortunate internees, my brethren, had been shipped from Hungary to their fateful destination. At least we were not crowded to the extreme in our wagons. We could lie down, use our personal bundles as pillows under our heads and were not mistreated by our guards. To be sure, we were hungry and tired, but that was a permanent state with us. It seemed to us that all mankind was starving, and that it was not possible that anyone could rest enough and satisfy his hunger. I made it a rule with me to eat my bread at once, because I did not wish to tempt any of my fellow inmates by the sight of my bread bulging from my bundle. I ate my bread and drank the water allotted to me, and then I tried to murmur a prayer, to think of the Lord, to ask for His assistance. I fell asleep rather easily, and slept sufficiently to refresh myself, in spite of the swaying of the train, the din caused by the rolling cars, the sighs of the men around me, in spite of the moans, the screams they uttered in their dreams.

After two days of the journey, we arrived at the Hungarian-Polish frontier. There we had to transfer to another train. One by one we alighted and stretched our legs. We were cold, numb from the long immobility, numb also in our souls. The cattle car had reduced our human sensitivity. We felt empty, indifferent to anything that was happening to the outside world, to what would happen to us. Or so we thought. Our insensitivity was at once shaken by the arrival of another long train of cattle cars completely sealed, filled with humans. Out of the sealed cars came voices of children; of women; of people gone insane; cries for help; screams; the sound of sobbing; the appeal of children for help for their mothers; the cries of victims who shouted that they were choking, who asked for air; a dissonance of lamentations recorded from the circles of Dante's Inferno, as it were. Never, whatever I saw, whatever I went through later on, did anything shake up my innermost being as much as this encounter with the invisible but highly audible fellow-sufferers. "Members of the human race" I thought, "are treated in this way by other members. Both the victims and the torturers are degraded. Mankind in its entirety is engulfed in a tidal wave of evil and crime that is sweeping away what so many generations have built up in terms of human solidarity."

It seldom happens to any human being that he suffers from the plight of others more than from his own personal woes. Yet this was what happened to most of us in those few moments while that train, filled with the doomed and the damned, rolled by before our eyes. My tears sprang forth abundantly, perhaps a reaction of nature to the burning, gnawing sensation inside my chest. The anguish of our helplessness was unbearable. We hurried to get into our own cattle cars in gloomy silence. I, descendant of rabbis, a rabbi myself, felt the weight of centuries of persecution of my people on my shoulders during those bitter minutes.

Jaramce was the name of the camp toward which we were directed, a foreign name which we had to learn. It remained indelibly imprinted in my memory because of the way it became, from a mere name, a living reality. As the letters spelling out that name leapt one by one into our field of vision, a terrible crash was heard. Our train was shaking, tilting, threatening to turn over. Then we felt as though the ceiling was collapsing, and again as though the bottom of the car was open under our feet. I felt like I was hit over my head by something dull, but tremendously powerful, stabbed in my sides by sharp knives. The door of the car opened under the shock; I jumped out, remained lying on the ground, stunned but unhurt.

Our train had collided with another one coming from the opposite direction. I saw many people running, gesticulating. I got up, looked inside the car. There lying on the floor, were bodies of those killed by the collision. Others had beeen badly injured. Everyone inside was terribly excited, and again I heard lamentations, moaning. The guards who were to receive us cursed. Stretchers arrived to take the dead and the injured away.

I said to myself that my leap out of the car, acting

upon an impulse, probably saved my life for I had been sitting in that part of the car that had been almost flattened by the collision. Once more a miracle occurred in my life. One of those events that unbelievers call a chance occurrence. I attributed it to the protection of God, and I addressed a silent prayer of thanks to the Almighty.

ESCAPE FROM SLAVERY

And call upon me in the day of trouble; I will deliver thee, and thou shalt honour me—Psalm 50:15.

A desolate landscape drenched by the sun, no trees anywhere, our camp was on flatland, isolated from the fields, from the villages. It had barracks of a uniform rust color; the houses of the guards on the edges of the camp; others for storage; a large ditch serving as a latrine, its stench offensive to our nostrils. Barbed wire surrounded the camp.

In the barracks we enjoyed the unheard-of luxury of wooden beds without mattresses, piled up on top of each other. There was also a heap of straw in a corner. It looked old, used. I preferred to do without it, afraid as I was of lice and bugs. I put my clothes on the bare wood. The nights were warm so that I did not need a blanket.

At daybreak, we aligned for the appeal. In that particular camp we were the only labor battalion. We numbered about one hundred fifty men. We received our ration of bread for the day, which I ate immediately. We were then marched to the warehouse to get our spades or other tools necessary for our daily work. Each of us was responsible for these, and we had to hand them in after the day's work.

Our labor consisted of digging ditches and erecting fortifications at a place distant about a mile and a half from the camp. I realized that an enemy army would have to come down on the plain from the slopes of the Carpathian Mountains for its invasion of Hungary. In this sense, sending out Hungarian labor battalions to Polish territory was justified, provided—and this seemeed to be the case—that the Poles themselves did not have the manpower to fortify their own country.

The daily march from the camp to our place of work was the only diversion in our otherwise unbearably dull life. At noon, we were given a thin soup from the mobile kitchen that was sent out for us. A half hour to eat and to rest and the work was resumed till sunset. Sometimes our guards authorized an extra half-hour rest in the afternoon on condition that our work assigned to us be completed by the end of the day. These guards were Hungarians themselves, foreigners in the country. They felt lonely and in the need of human communication. It was only with us, their prisoners, that they could speak at all, which brought about a certain relaxed atmosphere among us.

As one project was completed, we were sent out to other locations at a greater distance from our camp. We could then see from afar some villages peacefully huddling in the shade of a small wood. The peace of nature was in striking contrast with the nonsensical war that was raging in the world. The Polish peasants, men and women, looked very much like their counterparts in Hungary. I was digging ditches, day in and day out, and wondered about the sanity of mankind, about its inability to enjoy what nature had offered to it.

My hands holding the spade worked independently of my mind. My thoughts were from one point in time and space to another, embracing mankind, God and the Universe. My arms were just a machine, and I really lived in those days through my mind, in my contemplations.

In my thoughts I was with my wife, my son and my family; my imagination was so vivid that I actually saw them, talked to them. More than once, I was punished for my escape from the ugly reality; I was brutally recalled to it by one of the guards.

One day I received a tremendous blow on my back.

"Say, you pig, are you dreaming or what?" a voice thundered.

The guard had noticed that the ditch I was digging was not advancing fast enough. The heap of dirt around it was too small for him. He criticized the way I was holding the shovel.

"What was your occupation before we picked you up?" he inquired.

I told him that I was a rabbi. This answer amused him immensely.

"A rabbi, he is a rabbi!" he repeated laughing. He went to tell the news to his fellowguards, then he planted himself behind me. "So you were praying instead of doing honest work!" he said. He then egged me on to work faster and faster, until my pace of shoveling became frantic, he kicking and whipping me all the time. He finally got tired of mistreating me, and ordered me to pick up a heavy tree and run with it to the top of the mountain. I cannot understand how I managed to get there. I felt at first that my heart was falling out of my chest, then suddenly, a dull pain paralyzed me. It threatened to knock me down, it ran down to my legs; my lips became parched and I was totally shaken.

From then on, I tried to avoid that cruel guard whenever I could. Yet, if he happened to be in a bad mood, or set his eyes upon me, he started his scathing remarks about me.

"This do-nothing, the Rabbi! This phoney," he used to say. Then again, "How come you don't have a beard, you swine? Too bad, I would tear it out."

One day I suffered at his hand an ordeal that it is impossible for me to describe accurately. My tormentor must have been drunk, for he was in a particularly vicious and dangerous mood. He came to me and hit me with his fist, then with a stick.

"This is going to be your last hour, you bum!" he growled. "To the wall with you!"

He made me stand against the wall and said, "Now I will shoot you!"

He pulled a gun out of his belt and aimed it at me. I closed my eyes, tried to pray, but no words came to my mind. Suddenly, the images of my beloved emerged before my mind's eye.

"Oh Lord, accept my life as a sacrifice and spare them from similar agony. Lead them back to freedom!" These words were not articulated, rather thought in a flash. Everything was image and color in my inner world, colors and images that changed into each other, chased each other, independent of my will.

"I am going to die!" I heard a voice in the midst of this kaleidoscope, followed by a laugh. The sound of this laugh made me open my eyes.

"You are trembling, Jew!" the guard said, lowering his weapon. "Next time I'll finish you off." He grinned and departed. I must have been in an awful shape, for one of my fellow inmates came to me and wiped my face. Much later I learned that the guard who thus tortured me, subsequently joined the Communist Party, and was welcomed there.

Even among my fellow inmates, there were some who resented my prayers mornings and evenings. "Much good does it do for you!" they railed. It seemed to me that these men envied me for despairing less in our situation than they were, for keeping up some hope, and in spite of all, a sort of serenity. At least, looking back, this is how I can analyze their hostility to my saying of prayers. They called me a fool and also a fake, just as our guard did. Nevertheless, none of them denounced me. and with time, a few even started to speak to me in a friendly tone. The exhausting work and the insufficient food undermined my health. I felt constant fatigue, and fever alternating with chills. I was allowed to stay in our barracks for a few days. One morning, before the others aligned for the appeal, one of the men, a gaunt fellow with a pale complexion, eyes red from lack of sleep, came to my bed and handed me something wrapped in a piece of cloth.

"Take this," he said. "I saved it up yesterday for you."

It was a portion of his daily bread. I looked at him, not comprehending. Was there such a thing possible in a place like ours?

"I want you to have it," he repeated. "You need to get your strength back." He dropped the precious package into my lap and scurried out, not to be late to the appeal.

I learned that this generous benefactor of mine used to be the owner of a small grocery store in the outskirts of Cluj. His wife had been deported and he had not heard from her. Fortunately for them, they had no children. I prayed from then on every day for him and his wife. We became attached to each other in the subsequent weeks, till events separated us.

The high Jewish holidays came. We went out to our daily chores as usual. On the eve of the Day of Atonement, as we gathered in our barracks after work, I stepped forward and asked whether anyone wished to join me in the prayers appropriate on the occasion. I would recite them from memory, as we possessed no prayer books. To my surprise, eleven men replied in the affirmative. Three others volunteered to watch so that we should not be surprised by the guards. On that evening and on the following day no one, not even those known to be notorious unbelievers, uttered a single word of mockery or disapproval. The mood was sad but solemn; I noticed that most of my companions in suffering withdrew into themselves on that day, addicted to meditations. This, I said to myself, is the real meaning of Yom Kippur after all, the withdrawal into oneself. Such an attitude implies meditation, and meditation implies an élan towards God. Religion was not dead among us in spite of all the vulgarity and brutality that reigned in the outside world. On the contrary, deep down I believe each of us, even the professed unbelievers, reserved a corner for transcendence. Without belief and hope, none of us had a chance to survive. This was more important than a strong body and muscles.

Thus the days went by resembling each other in their monotony. It seemed to us at times that this life would go on without end, that there could be no change ever; we were to finish our earthly existence in this foreign land, in slavery. Was I born for this? I often asked, meditating.

The images of my beloved, my wife holding our baby in her arms, my mother and father looking at me from a distance, kept returning to my mind's eye. At times I felt an almost unbearable longing for them. I would have given my life just to see them, to speak to them once more, but most of the time these visions conveyed to me the hope and promise of reunion. It occurred to me that my strong will and longing could force our destiny, and that these apparitions actually foreshadowed our future. Armed with this hope of eventual reunion, I fought the voice that made suggestions to me in my loneliness, to give up, to renounce, perhaps to put an end to my days. I simply chased away any such impulses. I did not allow them to take hold of me.

One day an unexpected event brought tremendous excitement into our lives. A plane flew over our camp, passing at great speed. One of us recognized it. "It's Russian!" he exclaimed. "The Russians must be closing in on us!"

That night no one slept in the barracks. Till the late hours after the lights were extinguished, groups were discussing in whispered tones the news.

"The Germans are finished," some said. "The Red Army will soon be here. We shall be free!"

This conclusion filled my comrades with tremendous joy. It did not last, however, because one of them remarked, "It's not likely that the Hungarians and the Germans will simply let us go where we please. They will drag us along if they have to withdraw from here."

These words had the opposite reaction. General gloom settled on most faces.

"We should try to surrender to the Russians," someone opined.

"This would mean to exchange one slavery for another. We would still be prisoners then."

No one could offer any convincing conclusion, but the apathy and resignation that characterized our previous days were gone. We were alerted to the fact that a change was bound to occur in our lives very soon.

We were right in our supposition. One day in the month of September, the guards announced, "You must pack up. Tomorrow at dawn we will leave."

We learned that our camp was to be transferred back to Hungary. We received the great news with mixed feelings. We feared a return to the country of Endre and Baky, the likelihood of their finishing us off before the final defeat of Germany and her Hungarian ally. On the other hand, we rejoiced at the imminence of this defeat that was becoming obvious to all of us. The problem for us was to survive until the time of liberation. (At the time, indeed, we had no reason yet to regard the Russians otherwise than as liberators, because they combatted the Nazis.)

We were to make the journey from Jaramce to Hungary on foot, by forced marches. Daily we covered an average of twenty-five to thirty miles. We marched ten to twelve hours a day, resting only after complete darkness settled on the land. We spent our nights in the open fields, without shelter, in any kind of weather, in rain, heat or cold. Our feet were swollen, the soles of our feet full of blisters; most of us had to shed our shoes because they were full of holes, and so torn, that they no longer protected our feet. So we marched barefoot; marching became increasingly painful to us. We had little to eat and were continuously egged on to hurry. No wonder that so many of us were in a weak condition, several unable to continue. It must be said that the latter were not shot, as happened so often in similar conditions, but admitted to a hospital. I asked for the same favor, but my guards found that I was in a relatively good condition, able to go on. I thought then that I would never live to see the end of the journey. I could hardly move my feet; in fact every move was an ordeal for me. If, in the beginning of the war, anyone had told me what I was going to go through, I would have said that this would be impossible for me to bear; but, I presume, many hundreds of thousands of people could have said the same thing about themselves.

Toward the end of September or in the beginning of October, we arrived in Hungary. We traversed a territory that the Versailles Treaty had given, after World War I, to Czechoslovakia, and that had been returned by Hitler to Hungary.

As we advanced, there were many signs that the population expected the defeat of the Germans and their allies. We managed to talk to some people and were told that Rumania had already capitulated and joined the Western powers. Also, that the British and the Americans had opened a second front, and that their armies were advancing in Europe. These rumors wonderfully boosted our morale. I also observed that the population was on the whole sympathetic to us, that they expected great changes in the near future.

Toward the end of October, we reached the town of Hust. That town had, before the war, a large Jewish community. In the town we found several deserted synagogues and Jewish homes. In the synagogues the sacred scrolls of the Torah, together with many Jewish books of scholarship and prayers, were torn, mutilated, scattered on the floor. We viewed these profanities with sorrow and dismay, but we were unable to do anything about them.

We did not stay in Hust, just went through and continued our march. Toward the evening we reached a small village. By that time my physical condition had worsened considerably. In addition to my swollen feet, I developed a constant fever with swollen glands. I knew that, no matter how much I was resolved to oppose the strength of my faith to the suffering of my body, physically I might collapse. I asked therefore one of our supervisors to allow me to rest up during the night in one of the abandoned Jewish homes. He granted me this favor, which in itself was extraordinary.

As I entered one of the homes with some friends of the labor batallion, we again beheld sacred books spread all over the floor. I examined them and to my great surprise, I discovered the book of my wife's grandfather, who had been a prominent Jewish leader in Hungary, known for his piety, erudition and kindness. The fact that this holy book came into my hands at a time when I was despairing of being able to hold out any longer acted upon me as an elixir of life, renewing my strength, instilling new courage into my soul. Miracles are of diverse nature; they can be recognized by their effect on individuals. The appearance of those holy scripts emerging from nowhere, at a time when faith was trampled upon by would-be conquerors, when evil seemed to triumph, constituted certainly a miracle for me, even though no one else was aware of it. That night, stretching out my tired legs on a run-down sofa that no one had deigned to carry away, my mind was at rest and I slept the sleep of the just. I awoke refreshed, determined to go on. I kept the book of my wife's grandfather as a talisman; its powers protected me throughout those difficult times.

The next morning we had to move on. Reports had been received that the Russians were advancing very fast. We accelerated, if that was possible, our march and the guards saw to it that no one left the marching line. Germans joined the Hungarian guards commanding our Jewish Labor Battalion. It was clear to me that something decisive would soon happen to us, as the war was approaching its final phase. It was to be feared that, upon returning to Hungary proper, the Germans or their Hungarian acolytes would liquidate us in all haste. This fear was corroborated by the news, communicated to us by other labor battalions in the process of being repatriated, that the men admitted to hospitals during the previous days of our forced march had been picked up by Germans and deported. I once more realized my miraculous luck; had my request to be hospitalized been granted, I would now be on my way to Auschwitz or some other extermination camp!

On the same day that followed the discovery of the book written by my wife's grandfather, I received another piece of news. Someone told me that he had witnessed the departure of a special contingent of internees from Cluj to a foreign country. The contingent contained the members of my family. It was rumored that they were sent to Spain.

Much later, I learned that the real destination of that special contingent was Bergen Belsen, Germany. At the time however, it filled me with infinite joy and redoubled my courage. I decided that on the first occasion I would try to escape from the battalion.

The opportunity to do so presented itself to me sooner than I had expected. A farmer met our column coming from the opposite direction. I quickly asked him whether there was a road nearby that led to another village. Accosting an inhabitant of the places we were traversing was forbidden under penalty of being shot on the spot. Nevertheless, I had taken a chance, for I had decided to risk my life for my freedom. The farmer answered that there was a country road approximately half a kilometer away that led to a small village. I mentally weighed my chances of getting away without being noticed. I was in a state of euphoria, convinced that I would succeed. I had faced death on a number of occasions; all seemed to prove to me that a benevolent higher force was protecting me. Without this confidence in my destiny I could not have made that fateful decision, but I made it instantaneously without hesitation.

The road indicated by the farmer appeared. I quickly

ran away, and hidden behind a tree, I saw that I had not been missed. The column moved ahead; soon it disappeared from my sight. I was alone. I was free.

I wandered into a village, as I recall named Baning, formerly Czechoslovakia. All military forces, Hungarian or German, had been withdrawn from there. The villagers received me with open arms. I represented in their eyes a victim of the oppressors which they had learned to hate. I was in a state of complete exhaustion, badly undernourished, my hands and feet swollen, running a high fever. Truly I would not have lasted long had I not made my escape.

The priest came to see me and I told him that I was a rabbi who had escaped from forced labor. I asked him to help me in the name of God. The priest—his name was Mogyorosi—took me to his home, gave me light food and offered me a bed; then he called a physician. I remained under the latter's care for about a week.

My forces restored, I decided to return to Cluj, my native town. It was at a distance of about four hundred miles from the village. I took leave from my host, and from the friendly villagers. I promised to keep in contact with them through their priest, giving news about myself. Unfortunately, this was not possible because soon after my departure, the village was annexed by the Soviet Union, and cut off from all communications with the outside world.

The priest arranged for me a ride with a farmer who was going to Hust. His carriage, drawn by horses, was carrying vegetables to the market there. I was hidden under a heap of vegetables. Before we reached the town, I alighted from the carriage to avoid jeopardizing the safety of that kind farmer.

As I approached Hust on foot I was stopped by a Russian officer. He ordered me to follow him to the nearby military headquarters of the Russian army to work for them. I did not speak any Russian, but I could make myself understood in the Slovak dialect of the people of that region.

I explained to him that I had just escaped from a forced labor camp of the Nazis, and that I was not in a condition to do any menial work.

Far from sympathizing with my plight, his cold answer was, "Evrei ne rabota," which means, "The Jew does not want to work." He forced me to go with him, indicating by his gestures that he would shoot me if I refused.

I was still so weak, I could hardly stand on my feet. My heart was beating at the thought that from one slavery I was now falling into another; the new slavemasters did not seem to me any better than those I had escaped from. "You will not hold me!" I said to myself, and I determined that I would once more run away at the first opportunity.

The Russians put me to work at once. I had to carry on my shoulder sacks of corn or of wheat from one storehouse to another. I really thought I would collapse under the load. I had violent chest pains as though a thousand knives stabbed me at once from my shoulder down to my abdomen. Breathing caused me excruciating pain; the sweat was running in streams down my spine, along my cheeks. I had basically a healthy constitution and was quite robust by nature, but somehow the fatigue of past hardships, the emotional upsets, the worries and the grief, all that had undermined my strength. The few days spent in the village had somewhat restored my strength, but much less than I had thought. I needed time and rest to fully recuperate.

Fortunately for me, there was total disorganization at the place where I was working. After about an hour, I suddenly found myself unguarded. I left the sacks on the ground, and ran out of sight as fast as my legs could carry me.

I hid in the barn of a farmer till the night. When darkness fell, I set out toward my goal, Cluj. How I was going to get there without being caught by the Russians, I had no idea. I did not even know why I wanted to get to Cluj, since I had been told that my family was no longer there, but I hoped that I would meet old acquaintances in my home town, Jews and non-Jews who would help me help others. Also, I entertained the idea that perhaps from Cluj I would be able to go to the capital of Rumania and perhaps abroad.

I had a little money, given to me by Mogyorosi, the charitable priest of Baning. It helped me at the outset of my perilous journey to buy some food; some was also given to me by the peasants.

I met other former labor campers who were now heading home. They told me that they avoided capture by the Russians by giving the soldiers watches or anything valuable. One of them owed his freedom to the fact that he had been able to keep a small chain with a medallion that contained the picture of his mother. A Russian soldier took the medallion and returned the picture to him, letting him go free.

I traveled in the company of this man for about a week. It was easier for two to look around and watch, to inquire about the whereabouts of the Russians; also we shared with each other whatever we could get in the way of food.

After we parted company, I journeyed alone. I was now able to do some work on farms to earn shelter, a few eggs and some vegetables. In slow and cautious stages I thus advanced, crossing Hungary toward the territory now occupied by the Rumanian army. Indeed, the Rumanians had reoccupied the provinces they had held prior to Hitler's arbitration regarding Transylvania; Cluj was now under their control.

I crossed the border that separated the Hungarians from their Rumanian neighbors. A lonely traveler, with no other assistance than his will to survive and his faith in the Providence, in God, I looked back and I sighed with relief. I had come back from afar, from the depth of misery, from the threshold of death. The words of the Psalms escaped my lips in an irresistible, deep-felt prayer:

And call upon me in the day of trouble; I will deliver thee, and thou shalt honour me.

How differently the Rumanian army behaved from the Russians! An officer to whom I identified myself and told my story, gave me a paper that invited all Rumanian authorities to lend assistance to me. Soldiers gave me food, allowed me to travel with them on military vehicles; thus I reached Cluj some time in October, 1944.

The city offered the sight of unbelievable chaos. The hurricane of war had left in its wake nothing but devastation. My own and my parents' home had been utterly destroyed; what little furniture was left was ruined. Our library, composed before I left of more than two thousand volumes, was in shambles. The floors were littered with torn books. I could not salvage anything, for it was dangerous even to stay inside the house. The walls or the ceiling could collapse any minute.

Most of the once splendid synagogues were in ruins or were being used as depots. What had taken centuries to build, was maliciously, deliberately destroyed. Two savage armies had passed there: first the Hungarians then the Russians. They had faced each other, but they had behaved the same way. They had emptied not only the Jewish homes, but the entire city of anything valuable. The Russians, so-called allies, behaved just like their enemies. They were looting, stealing wherever possible. People were constantly on their guard; young girls and women were hastily sent out of reach of the soldiery. The Rumanian army had been ordered not to interfere with the activities of the Russians in order to avert any clash.

I had nothing but rags to cover my body. Where would I find some clothes? I remembered that, prior to my departure, we had buried in the Rabbinical College (which was our property), a few of our clothes in a large box. I went there and found a suit and an overcoat, along with a few shirts. I was transformed from a beggar and a tramp once more into a civilized human being.

Food and lodging were my next concern. One of my former neighbors, a Gentile, a fine decent man, offered me hospitality for a few days till I could formulate some plans concerning my future. I could only have one plan, namely that of retrieving my family. Concerning their whereabouts, I learned from various sources that indeed my wife and son, as well as my youngest sister were part of a special transport to Budapest. From there they had been taken to Germany, and then allegedly to Switzerland. This transport was the result of negotiations undertaken by Dr. Rudolf Kastner, for the purpose of saving as many Jewish lives as possible. These negotiations and their outcome constitute in themselves a much debated, important chapter of the history of World War II. They were carried on in haste, under the greatest pressure, for the Nazis were bent upon exterminating all the Jews in Europe. The fate of my family was intimately connected with their outcome.

JEWISH LIVES—MERCHANDISE FOR BARTER

Representatives of Zionist organizations led by two men, Dr. Rudolph Kastner and Joel Brand, had been active in Europe for some time prior to Hitler's occupation of Hungary. They pursued the task of saving as many Jewish lives as possible by any means at their disposal. They served as couriers transmitting messages between Poland, Slovakia and Turkey on the one hand, Switzerland and Hungary on the other hand. They were conducting negotiations with the occupying German power and saw to it that financial arrangements whenever they could be agreed upon, were carried out. They had done good work in Poland and in Slovakia. A small number of Jews there were released from concentration camps, and saved from deportation and the gas chamber thanks to their efforts.

In Hungary, Dr. Kastner and Joel Brand operated through an intermediary by the name of Joseph Winninger. A courier of the Reichswehr, Winninger also carried messages to and fro from Jewish organizations, and could be relied upon to implement banking operations. Through him, Dr. Kastner and Joel Brand contacted a liaison officer of the Reichswehr by the name of Dr. Schmidt. The latter informed them of an existing feud between the Reichswehr and the SS, and expressed the hope that the Reichswehr would gain the upper hand in the contest. This was of capital importance for the Jews, because the Reichswehr, the regular army, was known to be more humane than the SS, composed of Hilter's selected henchmen. Theretofore it was the SS that had planned the cruel persecution of Jews throughout Europe. It was under their supervision that their deportation had taken place.

Dr. Schmidt told the representatives of the Zionists that the Germans—meaning both the Reichswehr and the SS—would consider sparing the lives of Jews against a one-time payment of two million dollars. They would accept monthly installments, with a down payment of two hundred thousand dollars. This had been said to them prior to the German occupation of Hungary.

After the occupation, Dr. Kastner and Brand immediately got in touch with Winninger and Dr. Schmidt. In the beginning the negotiations were conducted in the presence of Winninger and Schmidt mainly through a certain Obersturmbannführer Krumey, an officer in the Reichswehr. However, the Jewish negotiators soon found out that they could do nothing without the consent of the SS, and that the fate of the Jews were principally in the latter's hands. From then on, representatives of the SS also participated in the negotiations in apparent harmony with the Reichswehr.

Parallel with the negotiations conducted by Zionists, other negotiations had been started by Phillip Freudiger, president of the Orthodox Jewish community in Budapest. Freudiger got in touch with a Baron Wysliceni, who was reputed to be a confident and adviser of Colonel Eichmann, head of the German administrative department in Hungary, dealing with the Jewish question.

It was intimated that a payment of two million dollars would actualy save the Hungarian Jews from deportation. The first installment of two hundred thousand dollars was raised and paid by the Jewish Council, and it was hoped at that point that indeed the entire Hungarian Jewry would be saved. This hope was shattered by the sudden occurrence of two events.

The first was the confiscation of all Jewish assets by the Hungarian government. This edict was published unexpectedly. It was so drastic that it did not allow any Jew to possess more than three thousand pengös in cash, a very small sum. From bank accounts only one thousand pengös per month could be withdrawn, provided this withdrawal did not raise the limit of three thousand pengös at the disposal of the owner of the account. Information was received to the effect that the Hungarian government would not release even a fragment of the considerable Jewish fortunes for the purpose of the construction of Jewish labor camps or Jewish welfare organizations of any kind.

With one blow, this edict of the Sztojay government reduced the Jews of Hungary to a state of beggary. The treasury of Jewish welfare organizations was empty. Recent anti-Jewish laws had deprived many of their livelihood. The assistance given to these people had drained the financial reserves of the Jewish community. With the bank accounts frozen, the Jewish businesses closed or confiscated, Jews prevented from earning anything, they ceased to have any income. Jews only possessed whatever they had been able to conceal with the help of friendly, cooperative non-Jews. All valuables still possessed by Jews, gold and precious gems, works of art of any kind, Oriental rugs or anything else, could be sold by them only at prices representing a fraction of what they would have fetched before the occupation of the country by the Nazis. As most of the Jews were penniless, only small amounts of money could be raised for the purpose of the negotiations. Yet the plan of saving the Jews from annihilation by means of paying a ransom to their tormentors required a well-filled treasury.

The second event was even more fateful from the point of view of the salvation of the unfortunate Hungarian Jews. Dr. Schmidt, who conducted negotiations with Dr. Kastner and Joel Brand, was of course aware of Wysliceni's parallel negotiations with Freudiger. Was he jealous of Wysliceni, or did he act out of other considerations? The fact is that he seemed to report to Eichmann that the two million dollars asked for ransom was too low, and that much higher amounts could be squeezed out of the Jews in Hungary. Wysliceni was thereupon dismissed as a negotiator and Eichmann took over the negotiations personally. He had Winninger and Dr. Schmidt arrested, and Krumey, the most decent among the lot, was bypassed.

Previously the negotiators agreed that six hundred fifty persons who had their immigration certificate to Israel would be allowed to leave. Later, this figure had been raised to seven hundred fifty. Shortly after Eichmann replaced the two other Germans, he reported that the immigration of these people to Israel became impossible because of an agreement the Germans had with the representatives of Arab states not to allow any Jews to emigrate to Israel. Thereupon another plan emerged, that of letting the Jews in unlimited numbers emigrate to South America, or in a roundabout way, to Israel. In exchange, the Germans were to receive important deliveries of war and raw materials.

This plan was probably prompted by the desperate need of the Germans to replenish their stores of war and raw materials depleted by the devastating bombardments by the Allies. Such materials had at that time much greater value for the Germans than cash or other valuables. Eichmann allegedly declared, "For each truck you can have one hundred Jews."

Around the middle of April in this year of 1944, the northern, eastern and southwestern border areas of Hungary were declared areas of war operations. This coincided with the concentration of the Jews of those areas in ghettos.

The Germans had demanded the concentration of Jews in ghettos only in the areas of operations. Endre, the undersecretary of the Sztojay government, issued orders on his own responsibility to round them up everywhere in the country with the exception of Budapest, and to concentrate them in designated places as a prelude to their deportation.

We must repeat in this connection that the non-Jewish Hungarian population witnessed the suffering of their fellow citizens with complete passivity. To understand their attitude, one must refer to the anti-semitic propaganda of the past fifty years which was further kindled and carried to a high pitch by the newspapers since the German presence in the country. Also to intimidation: whoever dared to put in a good word for his Jewish neighbor or friend, or for a relative who happened to be Jewish, was vilified and threatened. The members of the Hungarian Arrow-Cross Party, a counterpart of the German Nazi Party, watched with the vigilance of bloodhounds so that no help was extended to the people concentrated in the ghettos.

While these events occured in the provinces, Freudiger, representative of the Orthodox Jews in Budapest, asked Eichmann what the purpose of the concentration of the Jews was. Eichmann assured Freudiger that they would be transferred to Germany to work camps, and that this transfer would affect only three hundred ten thousand people (he spelled out the number) while the rest of the Jews could go free provided that the negotiations conducted by the Zionists and the Jewish representatives in Budapest were concluded in a satisfactory manner.

It is necessary to open here a parenthesis to occupy ourselves with the personalities of the two Zionist representatives, Dr. Kastner and Joel Brand.

I knew Dr. Kastner; he was an attorney and an editor of a daily newspaper, an idealist and gifted man of great qualities. He was ready to assume a personal risk for the accomplishment of a task he had set for himself. However, there was also a tendency in him to bypass anyone who would hinder his efforts. He was a stickler in keeping appointments and agreements. He was a Zionist of the utmost devotion and a politician of the first order, liable to see every occurrence from a political point of view.

In view of the above traits in his character, it is not unlikely that Dr. Kastner was anxious to be the principal artisan in the shaping of the destinies of almost one million Hungarian Jews. In order to hold all the affairs and concentrate them in his own hands, he took the work that several people would have been incapable of handling, upon himself.

Joel Brand was a man of smaller caliber whose abilities did not match those of Dr. Kastner, but he was perhaps more practical in certain areas than the latter.

These were the two men who negotiated with Eichmann at the critical moment when three hundred thousand Hungarian Jews faced the immediate prospect of deportation, and when the already mentioned plan of saving them by paying for their freedom with the deliveries of war materials and raw materials useful for the German war economy was discussed.

The negotiators asked Eichmann to order that the deportations of the Jews concentrated in the provinces be suspended till an agreement was reached. He refused. "I must get tough with the Jews or the Jewish organizations abroad will believe that they can get concessions from me anyway," he allegedly declared to Joel Brand.[*]

Even if he had acceded to the requests of the Jewish representatives, the lives of the Jews of the Hungarian provinces would have remained threatened just the same, because Endre and Baky worked at that time at cross purposes with the Germans. They were not concerned about bargains benefiting the German war machine. In their implacable hatred, they wanted to complete the extermination of the Jews within the shortest possible period. Nevertheless, Eichmann's refusal to suspend the deportations sealed the fate of those unfortunate people.

Meanwhile, the negotiations with Eichmann had advanced to the point where he understood the necessity to send representatives of the Jews abroad to contact the

---

[*] Alex Weissberg: *Desperate Mission*. Joe Brandt's story as told by Alex Weissberg, translated from German by Constantine Fitz Gibbon and Andrew Foster-Mellior (New York, Criterion Books, 1958).

world Jewish organizations with a view of obtaining from these, binding agreements concerning the delivery of war materials. Eichmann still had in his cards the lives of six to seven hundred thousand Jews.

He designated Joel Brand to go to Turkey for the purpose just mentioned, and he was to be accompanied by a certain Bandi Grosz, a man of the Hungarian Intelligence Service who was supposed to keep an eye on Brand's activities.

The members of the Jewish Council informed of Eichmann's decision were greatly upset. They believed that he, Brand, did not have the qualities necessary to carry out such a grandiose mission, the saving of seven hundred thousand lives through diplomacy. They thought that they could have proposed to Brand, had Kastner kept them informed of the progress of his negotiations, men more capable to carry the negotiations to a successful conclusion. It was generally believed that Eichmann had chosen Brand and not Dr. Kastner, because he thought that he could get a better bargain through him than he could through Kastner. Little did the members of the Jewish Council know about the international situation, or about the mentality of the Allied leaders and the factors that influenced the latter's decisions in the matter of the saving of the Jews of Europe.

Brand departed on May 15, 1944, just about the time when the first deportations in the northeastern areas of Hungary took place. Perhaps the coincidence of the two facts had been planned.

By the 10th or the 12th of June, the entire contingent of three hundred ten thousand people had been deported. At the end of May, the concentration of the Jews of Budapest was ordered. The council was given the assignment to prepare a plan of concentration.

It was generally assumed that the British and the Americans would not bomb the parts of the city inhabited by Jews. They established therefore, so-called Jewish houses in all sections. The Gentile residents had to move out of those houses. The Jewish population of the capital numbered about two hundred thousand which meant that they had to move into three thousand five hundred houses. This mass moving was to be completed within six weeks.

Undersecretary Endre found this delay too long and wrote across the document, without reading the plan to the end, "2500 houses, 2 days." It was only with the greatest effort that the Council obtained an extension to seven days, with the number of houses increased to two thousand seven hundred. Even the five extra days did not suffice to carry out the mass transfer of people, and a further delay of three days was conceded out of necessity.

In the first days of July, the deportation of the Jews was begun in the outskirts of Budapest. These industrial suburbs had a relatively large Jewish population. About twenty-three thousand of them were taken to a brickyard in Békásmegyer, after being robbed of their possessions. For five days these people, who had spent their days and nights without shelter, received not a piece of bread nor a drop of water. Characteristic of the sadism shown by the gendarmes toward their helpless victims is the following, testified to by the survivors of those horrible times.

The large cemeteries, whether Jewish or non-Jewish, of the capital were situated outside of the administrative district of Budapest, in Rákoskeresztur. One day, the entire personnel of the two Jewish cemeteries were arrested and interned. Those were the days when, as a result of the tremendous bombardments of the city, hundreds of bodies were awaiting burial since there were not enough gravediggers to attend to the job. People who came to the cemetery for the funeral of their relatives were admitted to the cemeteries. Then when they left, they were arrested by the gendarmes who were waiting for them. They were immediately taken to the internment camps to be deported.

The deportations and the brutality with which they were carried out could not be concealed from the non-

Jewish population. One could not let hundreds of thousands of people disappear without a trace in a small country go unnoticed. The people who had traveled in the provinces and returned to Budapest were talking. The incidents they related, often from eyewitness accounts, coupled with the reports of steady progress by the Allies in the war, provoked great nervousness in the capital. People began to understand that no self-respecting nation can deny responsibility for such cruelty as was shown by the Hungarian authorities in the execution of the German orders. The occupants, with their small forces, would never have been able to bring about the rapid concentration and deportation of so many people had the Hungarian authorities not shown their zeal and enthusiasm for this plan. People were afraid of the reprisals of the victors after the war. Rumors circulated to the effect that Budapest was destined to be erased by Allied bombers as a punishment for the crimes against the Jews.

The government of Hungary, cognizant of the atmosphere created by the stunning tragedy of the Jews, started a propaganda campaign to reassure the population. The newspapers were informed that the Jews who had been deported were taken to places of settlements, and that they were given the opportunity of doing work useful for the community. Reports from villages and cities which had been cleared of their Jewish residents, declared that the deportation of the Jews had been carried out in the most humane manner. There were pictures of the villagers overjoyed at being freed from the Jews who had exploited them. In spite of this propaganda, the nervousness of the people increased, especially after the forces of General Eisenhower opened the second front and advanced in Brittany.

Days and weeks passed and the Jewish Council, and indeed the entire Jewish population still alive, awaited with great anxiety the outcome of the negotiations between Eichmann and the Jewish organizations abroad. From Joel Brand came news that things were going well, and that he would soon, in possession of the necessary authorizations, return with binding engagements on the part of the Allies. The mood of hope was soon followed by one of the greatest pessimism, as the deportations continued unabated, as no Jewish family was not mourning some or several losses of beloved members, as every Jew in the country trembled for his life, as every hour, every minute brought them closer to certain annihilation.

Telegrams and letters came, but no Brand!

Rumors continued to follow in frequent succession. Brand was allegedly in Palestine. Brand was on his way to Budapest via Lisbon. He was unable to come and had sent a delegate from Istanbul in his place who was bringing with him contracts specifying the places of delivery of war materials in exchange of Jews.

The rumors were flying, and the deportations continued inexorably. Brand was supposed to have reached England to discuss the emigration of Hungarian Jews with British and American authorities. Brand had left and was waiting in Lisbon for his return visa to Hungary.

The confusion and anxiety of the people increased. They felt entrapped, helpless. As each day passed, they believed less and less in their eventual salvation.

Kastner, who had taken everything upon himself without being authorized to by the Hungarian Jewish leaders, now had to admit that sending Brand abroad was a disaster for the Jews of Hungary. Anxious to save what he could, he made Eichmann the offer of raising money, and securing precious stones and foreign currency in case he, Eichmann, ordered a suspension of the deportations. Eichmann refused, still maintaining the deportations would spur the Jewish world organizations to hasten the deliveries he needed.

Blood for money, money for blood, was his motto.

Nevertheless, he consented to operate on the basis of an "open account," that is to say, to release a given number of Jews against a given amount of money or valuables. Dr.

Kastner thereupon, in cooperation with the Jewish Council and Mr. Freudiger, concentrated on saving the lives of prominent Jews, or their families interned in the camps of the provinces. These people were to be taken out from the camps and brought to Budapest. Kastner himself hailed from Cluj, the Hungarian Kolozsvár. After long bargaining with Eichmann, he succeeded in saving three hundred eighty persons in that city. It was agreed that these people would be taken to a special camp in Budapest, administered by the Jews themselves. In case negotiations with foreign Jewish organizations were successfully concluded, they, the inhabitants of these special camps, were to be the first to be allowed to depart.

I pieced this information together after my return to my native town. Of course, all this was conjecture for I knew nothing certain at that time about the whereabouts of my family. I had only the rumors that they were included in the special arrangement worked out by Dr. Kastner with Eichmann. To communicate with the outside world, perhaps even to leave the country, I had to get to Bucharest, capital of Rumania.

I could do nothing without money, and I had none. I contacted a Rumanian physician, a friend of our family, to whom we had entrusted some jewelry for safekeeping. He showed me his house; it had been looted by the Russians of anything that had the slightest value. The drapes had been removed, the wardrobes emptied, the lingerie vanished. He and his wife had been left with nothing but the clothes on their bodies.

"My dear friend," he said embarrassedly, "we have become partners in poverty."

He examined me and gave me medical aid, as much as was possible under the circumstances. He could not even invite me for dinner; there was hardly enough food for him and his family.

I left him more sorry for him than for myself. I knew that whatever the obstacles, I would get some money to go to Bucharest, capital of the country, in order to obtain a passport, to leave the country, to search for those who must be waiting for me and whom I longed so much to clasp to my heart.

BUCHAREST—I RECEIVE A DIPLOMATIC PASSPORT

I returned from the house of my impoverished physician to that of my former neighbor with whom I was lodging. I told him what I had just seen and heard regarding the behavior of the Russian "ally." He frowned and said, "Man does greater harm to man than any disaster nature may send upon him. We live in the war zone here, and the law no longer protects us. Society has disintegrated. No one can hope to be spared; our very clothes may be snatched from our bodies. The lawlessness of the jungle reigns."

He reflected, looked me over, then added, "I feel deeply ashamed when I look at you. I feel guilty for what my fellow Hungarians have done to you. Yes, I feel guilty because everyone is his brother's keeper. You bear on your face the suffering you have been through. Our leaders have disgraced us. I, a lonely individual, feel like burying my face in ashes, like closing my eyes to the devil's work that is being done around us, but I would like to persuade you that there are still Hungarians who believe in human decency, and condemn what has been done in their name.

"The Russians have descended upon us like a cloud of crickets, devouring everything in their passage. They constitute our punishment. We must accept them in that spirit. They will pass, and what has been devastated, we will have to build up again."

He embraced me and offered me money.

"Take it," he said, "with you. This money will serve a good purpose. Perhaps it will help you get back to civilization and retrieve your family. I'd rather give it to you than be forced to give it to some Cossack who may ransack my house tomorrow."

His words moved me deeply. I said to myself, "To condemn all Hungarians is a generalization which may lead us to some unjust conclusions for what a number of them have done. Did not God say about Sodom and Gomorrah: 'I will not destroy it for the ten's sake' (Genesis 26:33). To condemn collectively any people is to follow in the footsteps of Hitler. This does not behoove a true Jew nor a true Christian. This Hungarian friend of mine has taught me what it means to be just and wise, which is the same thing as to be an enlightened human being."

I left Cluj for Bucharest by train in the morning of the next day, a war train used mostly by Russian military, with a sprinkle of civilians. For me it was a luxury train. Sitting on the wooden bench, my coat neatly folded in the net, comfortably leaning against the back of the compartment, I enjoyed the pleasant temperature within. I conjured up the vision of that other voyage in a cattle car I had made not so long before. Which one was the dream and which one was the reality, this train or that other one? Can the memory of a real event become a nightmare? Subsequent years answered this question emphatically in the affirmative. . . .

I was absorbed in my thoughts. Suddenly, a voice addressed me in Yiddish. How did he know I was a Jew? The question appears to me superfluous. My features, my eyes, the hesitant anxious moves of my limbs, everything revealed me to a fellow Jew. He wore the uniform of a Russian officer. I was startled. So there were some of our people among them too. So we could not think of the Russians either simply as "they," as a formless collective!

He asked me where I had come from, and where I was

going. I trusted him and spoke to him openly. I told him that I was a refugee from a labor camp, a rabbi.

"Do not stay in Rumania," he volunteered. "You may be prevented from exercising your profession. You may even lose your freedom again."

"Why? I haven't committed any crime. . . ."

He shrugged his shoulders, made a large gesture with his hands, his mouth twitched a little, but he gave no answer. His sign language spoke, however, eloquently to me. That man wanted to convey to me the truth that as long as I lived under Russian occupation, I as a Jew, had to fear the future, that I was not safe any time. It was a fraternal warning coming from someone who knew. I did not have to be told since the very purpose of my trip to Bucharest was to secure a passport and a visa, to get out into the free world. Nevertheless, the warning constituted an eye-opener for me. It taught me that the Communists were not merely anti-religious, but especially anti-Jewish for the same reason that Hitler was, namely that we are essentially a people living in the spirit. That the only Lord we recognize is the Lord of Heavens, and we are not to be reduced to mere objects. Ever since that conversation I have associated the concept of God with that of true spiritual and individual freedom, provided we accept the God within us with joy, and model our conduct according to His dictates. . . .

I changed the subject, and asked him to tell me something about Jewish life in Russia. To my amazement, he frowned and remarked simply, "I am a Russian officer."

This was an answer that was no answer which, however, I understood completely. It still further completed the line of my previous thoughts. I again changed the subject, spoke of trivial things and we parted in a friendly way.

It was the end of October or maybe the beginning of November of the year 1944.

Bucharest was beautiful in the fall. The sun illuminated the wide boulevards, the ornate palaces of the inner city. It felt good to see that apparently the war had not brought about the same chaos, the same disorganization there which I had seen in Cluj and the territories I had left behind. It was clear to me that the Rumanian government was still in control, in spite of the Russian occupation. The Rumanians were still masters at home, but there was the ominous and ubiquitous presence of the Russian military. Immediately after my arrival I could observe Russian soldiers, including officers, standing for many long minutes in front of the show windows of shops, admiring the abundance of merchandise displayed there. I noticed that the majority of them were not of European origin. I saw Kalmucks, Tatars and other Asiatic types with jutting cheekbones and small, sometimes slanted eyes. Most of them were of small stature, but a few were giants. They looked awkward and moved clumsily, suspiciously—so it seemed to me. They were particularly attracted by the sight of dishes in the windows of restaurants. They could hardly tear themselves from the spot. Of course, only their officers dared to enter.

In view of the occupation, the city was overcrowded and the hotels were full. In vain I searched for a room all evening. Finally, despairing, I put down my small bundle in the lobby of the Hotel Continental and told the porter that I was incapable of moving on; he would have to put me somewhere. I related to him part of my adventures of the recent past, and asked him to do what he could for me. Thereupon, he had a bed placed into one of the smaller drawing rooms of the hotel and put me up.

During the night I was frequently awakened by shootings, I found out later on that the Russian soldiers amused themselves by shooting in the air. They went on a rampage under the cloak of darkness, raping any woman they encountered, looting stores and taverns, breaking into homes, and stripping people in the streets of everything but their shirt and underwear.

As I had a hard time falling asleep after such interruptions, I reflected on what I would or could do to sustain myself and to work toward the aim I had set for myself.

I remembered the names of a few old friends of my family who had known my father and grandfather, and who had held the name "Glasner" in great respect. Many had remembered my grandfather, who admonished the Jews of Europe that a time would come when they would wish to leave for Palestine. "The time is now," he used to say, "while the doors of Palestine are still open." He predicted that one day the Jews would be prevented from settling in their promised homeland. My grandfather himself had followed his own advice and emigrated to Palestine in 1920. Many of my coreligionists were able to leave northwestern Transylvania before its annexation to Hungary; some settled in Bucharest where the authorities showed a more tolerant attitude toward the Jews. From the distance of long years past several names suddenly re-emerged in my memory. I knew that most of them had done well, and I had no doubt that they would help me in my present predicament. Also, I was hopeful that from Bucharest I would be able to contact my sister, Esther, married to Daniel Lewenstein before the war, who was established in Switzerland.

Thanks to the Jewish congregation of the city, it was not too difficult to find the people in question. I was not disappointed. The name "Glasner" still exercised the old spell on them. I was received with open arms and was given financial aid. Thanks to them, I found lodgings and was put in a position to concentrate on efforts to get in touch with my sister, and through her, to retrieve the traces of my family in Switzerland.

Bucharest, in fact the whole of Rumania, constituted at that time the last refuge for Eastern European Jews, offering them a degree of security. In 1941 and 1942 the Rumanian government, yielding to Nazi pressure, had consented to the deportation of some one hundred eighty-five thousand Jews from the northeastern provinces of Bucovina and Bessarabia to primitive camps in the Ukraine, which was then occupied by the Germans. However, at the very time when Hungary wholeheartedly and ferociously cooperated with the Nazis in the work of exterminating her Jewish population, Rumania changed her attitude toward the Jews. Not only did she refuse to deport more of them, but she even brought back forty-five thousand, returning them to their former homes. She also received those who had escaped from Hungary to Rumanian territory, did not intern them, and helped them in every way.

The merit for this humanitarian and courageous attitude must be ascribed to young King Michael. He was opposed to any deportation of Jews from Rumania. It was related to me by well-informed men in Bucharest that Prime Minister Antonescu would have refrained from the deportation of Jews in the first place if the Allies had made a strong appeal to him to that effect. Indeed, Antonescu, a general, was aware of the military potential and military reality, namely of the overwhelming superiority of the Allies in manpower, raw materials and technology. He realized that it would bring about their final victory. He feared reprisals on the part of the Allies for any war crimes committed in his name. One decisive appeal by a determined Allied statesman, and one hundred eighty-five thousand Jewish lives would have been saved.

I relate the above to describe the atmosphere that I found upon my arrival in Bucharest. The officials were ready to help me willingly if not ostentatiously. Still another fortunate circumstance greatly favored me. The former prime minister of Rumania, Tatarescu, knew me personally, for he had visited Cluj some years before, and on behalf of the Jewish community of the city, I had extended our welcome to him. Moreover, the renown of our family was known to him. I presented myself to him and he received me cordially. He recommended me to the Foreign Ministry without the help of which I could not establish contact with my sister in Switzerland. The Ministry transmitted a telegram to her, informing her of my presence in Bucharest, and inquiring about my family.

A few weeks later, the answer came which also was

transmitted to me through the Foreign Ministry. My brother-in-law advised me that my parents had safely arrived in Switzerland, but my wife and son had been retained in Bergen Belsen, Germany. As to my other sister, Naomi, married and residing before the war in Oradea-Mare, they had no information.

Anyone can imagine my feelings when I read the telegram: joy to learn that my dear father, mother and sister were safe; immense worry about my wife and little son who still remained in the clutches of the Nazis.

There was nothing I could do further except contact the Rumanian and International Red Cross. I hoped to be able to leave the country as soon as possible, but since this was not an easy matter, I decided to use the time of waiting to do something for my fellow refugees.

Most of them were destitute, demoralized, physically weak. They needed help. I volunteered my services to the Jewish organizations to bring moral and material relief to these refugees. It was immensely satisfying to me to be on the giving, on the helping side after having been helped myself. Each piece of bread that was handed out, each lodging secured, each medical examination given, each piece of information concerning dispersed members of the families obtained through my intermediary services, constituted on my part an act of thanksgiving for my own and my parents' survival, a prayer for my eventual reunion with all my beloved. Again, I must emphasize, action and praying were one and the same for me.

In the course of my contact with refugees freed by the advance of the Russian armies, I learned what I had feared from the beginning: the battalion of labor campers who had been with me in Jaramce, Poland, perished almost to the last man. As the Hungarian guards were replaced by Germans, the latter, impatient with the slow advance of the battalion, liquidated it and left with their wagons lest they be overtaken by the advancing Russians. Once more, I asked what force made me escape from the marching column, and what made my escape succeed? The word "luck" certainly does not give a satisfactory answer. . . .

I was lodged with a Jewish family who had a daughter, about twenty years of age. Living with them gave me an insight into the indoctrination of youth by the Communists. (Communist influence grew as the victories of the Red Army over the Germans became known in the country.)

One day the daughter informed her parents that she had joined the Communist Party. In vain the parents objected, but she coldly rebuffed them, telling them to mind their own business. Subsequent to joining the Party, she became increasingly estranged from her family. In fact, the Party replaced the role of her family in her eyes. To the Party she transferred her emotions and loyalty. Still the daughter refused to leave home as her father repeatedly asked her to do, because she tried to impose her own views upon her parents. It was interesting for me to hear her opinion about her own government and about the Allied leaders. She condemned General Radescu, the prime minister, for his "bourgeois" and "reactionary" attitudes in his relations with the Soviet Union. As to the Allied leaders, she spoke in derogatory terms of Churchill and praised President Roosevelt. She voiced the opinion that after Yalta, Churchill had been reduced to a secondary role, that he and the British in general no longer had much influence. There was a feeling, she said, that if any need arose to intervene with the Russian Military Command, this should be done through the American mission, not through the British, for the latter were disliked by the Russian authorities in Rumania. It was rumored that something had happened in Yalta that had offended the Russians, and the fault was Churchill's. She, and I understood the Communists, favored Roosevelt as the man to deal with on the side of the Western Allies; he alone had the power to make binding decisions.

Politics were rather confusing at that time. Rumors were constantly afloat. The defeat of Germany had become a foregone conclusion, admitted by everyone except the most fanatic Nazi sympathizers.

By chance I met the father of Anna Pauker during my stay in Bucharest. Anna was a well-known Communist leader, one of the earliest and staunchest supporters of Stalin. She had gone into exile in Russia at a time when Rumania, her native country, still enjoyed its independence; she returned with the arrival of the Red Army. From her exile she sent clandestine instructions to the Rumanian Communist Party. After her return, her influence in the Party was predominant, even though, officially, she held no position therein. Her job was, as subsequent events proved, to prepare the Party for the take-over of the state. Afterwards, when that became an accomplished fact, she was named Foreign Minister in the Communist government. She was responsible for the forced abication of the King, but her services, like those of so many members of the initial General Staff of international communism, were ill-rewarded. In 1952, Anna Pauker was implicated in the mass trials ordered by Stalin. She was arrested and jailed. Like other Jews, such as Slansky and Loebl in Czechoslovakia, she was accused of being an agent of international Zionism and Israel. Her fate constitutes a further proof of what is today common knowledge, that Jews who had adhered to the Communist parties and acceded to high positions, never were immune to suspicion and religious prejudice on the part of their comrades. Anna Pauker's name does not even appear in recent Communist encyclopedias, in spite of the important role she had once played in the building-up and strengthening of international Communism. The Communists punish those they repudiate by making of them non-persons, trying to delete their memory from history and certainly from the minds of the people.

Anna Pauker's father was a religious Jew who deeply deplored the activities of his daughter. He complained to me that he had tried to see her after she returned to the country, but she refused to receive him. Anna was thus demonstrating that she had broken with her family, because family ties and religion represented reactionary sentiments in her opinion. However, it takes two to be assimilated anywhere, with any nation and any movement: one who wishes to be assimilated and the others. The Communists, particularly the Russian Communists, and today the Communist parties obedient to the Soviet Union, are, we repeat, far from free from religious prejudice.

Meanwhile, I continued to be active in humanitarian and religious enterprises. I was instrumental in the formation of a union of refugee rabbis, who were saved from destruction by Hitler. Throughout these days, while awaiting a new decisive turn in my own fate, I was guided by an anecdote told me once by my late father (may he rest in peace). A sainted rabbi was approached by a man who had strayed away from religion. The man said, "Rabbi, I repent my sinful past and would like to atone for it. What shall I do? How shall I begin?"

The Rabbi answered, "Remember three things. First, there is only one man to do a certain job. Second, there is only one job to be done at a time. Third, there is only one day to do it."

This little story acted upon me the way the pragmatic philosophy of Seneca or Schopenhauer's maxims for the conduct of life would act on a receptive reader. I said to myself that a certain task was incumbent upon me every day, that it had to be done on that particular day, and that I alone, not anyone else, was responsible for carrying it out. As things evolved, there was a great deal to do. Our primary problem was: what could we do for the safety and welfare of the refugees who had come to Bucharest? Further, we had to turn our attention to the refugees who had been freed in Eastern Germany by the red armies. Reports received from those regions indicated that these unfortunate people were not aided by the Russians, and as a result, many died after they had regained their freedom. In fact, we learned that as a matter of policy, the Russians were disinterested in the fate of the former inmates of concentration camps. The giant who, with one hand, dealt hard blows to his staggering enemy, was not dealing out bread, shelter, medical aid and other necessities to the victims of the same enemy.

I recommended to our rescue committee that we urgently seek an audience with Andrei Vishinsky, deputy foreign minister of the Soviet Union. He was a frequent visitor to Bucharest, as well as to other capitals in the Danube Basin, actually traveling from one to the other at the time. Future events proved that the purpose of Vishinsky's travels was to implement a plan, worked out after the Yalta meeting of the Allied chiefs, which was to transform the countries in that region into Communist states in order to maintain them within the Russian sphere of influence.

At the end of December, 1944, I received a second telegram through the intermediary of the Rumanian Foreign Ministry. My wife and son had safely arrived in Switzerland. This was the most exalting moment of my life, reward for the suffering I had undergone. Overwhelmed with joy, it freed my mind from a constant preoccupation; it was now much easier for me to devote my efforts to the immediate tasks ahead of us.

My proposal was received by the Committee. We secured the services of a Jewish attorney raised in Russia, who was to function as our spokesman and interpreter. He prepared a detailed memorandum concerning the problem of the refugees in the Russian-occupied territories, as well as our suggestions as to how to lend them urgent assistance. Rescue squads would visit those regions, bringing with them food and medicine which we offered to provide. This was a first step in the relief program.

Mr. Vishinsky was noncommittal. He declared that he would take the memorandum to Moscow for study and would advise us. We left his office rather depressed. I personally was convinced that nothing would come out of our efforts to get relief to our coreligionists in their plight through the help of the Russians. My pessimism was justified. Vishinsky's answer is still pending.

An important meeting of Jewish religious leaders of Transylvania was held soon after in Bucharest. The subject discussed was the rebuilding and revival of Jewish life in West Transylvania. The survivors from Nazi camps returning home were in need of spiritual guidance. Both the rabbis and lay leaders pledged their efforts to further this aim. They agreed to call a convention in Cluj, and asked me, as the former deputy chief rabbi of that City, to open the meeting and to extend the greetings to the convention.

A few months had passed since my arrival in Bucharest after having escaped from a Nazi labor camp. Personally I had every reason to be satisfied with the results of my efforts during those months.

I had succeeded in obtaining information regarding my family. From a human wreck, I re-emerged a man solidly planted in the soil, able not only to take care of himself, but also to join in the rehabilitation of others. I was of course deeply grateful to Him who had preserved me during the cataclysm of the recent past and preserved those so dear to my heart. And above all, I was bathing, as it were, in a new light that is difficult for me to explain. In the midst of the general chaos, while war was still raging, when destruction caused by men was universal, I perceived inside me a strength of will, a joy and happiness that had nothing to do with earthly considerations. I had gained an insight into the divine in man, into the greatness that exists in everyone of us, but which is concealed by the shortsightedness of our daily existence, by our struggle for material goods and for power.

Truly, I can say that I was a new man, matured by suffering and the sight of suffering, as I was back in Cluj in May, 1945. The city where I had spent my childhood, where I had returned in search of my past, had been extraordinarily transformed during my short absence. New people with new, mostly confused ideologies had seized the levers of command, eager to transform the existing institutions in a hurry. They were insulting, intimidating, bullying, browbeating those whom they deemed to be too slow in adopting their new ways. Irresistibly I was reminded of the Nietzschean phrases of "God is dead" and "the reevaluation of all values."

The local Communist Party had a Jewish section, a contradiction in itself, for Communism professes to ignore religious distinctions. The leaders of that section opined that I was a reactionary; consequently they decided that they would not permit me to deliver the welcoming address to the Assembly. I insisted, on the other hand, on my rights as deputy chief rabbi, head of the Jewish community in the absence of my father. I was theatened with violent demonstrations, even with violence against my own person, if I did not step aside. I refused to yield to these pressures. My position was supported unanimously by the delegates from eastern Transylvania, and I prevailed, opened the meeting and was in command of the convocation till the meeting was turned over to the permanent chairman.

Thinking of that, my first brush with the Communists, I say to myself that at no time had I reflected on the possible reprisals my inflexible attitude toward them could have entailed. Looking back, I realize why they had yielded on that occasion. They were not yet sure of their strength. They could not declare themselves openly; they had to bide their time. Nevertheless, from a number of facts, from hints given to me by my former friends and followers, I realized that they were out to get me and that my life was in danger. This was an additional factor that prompted me to seek the opportunity to leave Rumania as fast as possible. This was henceforth a constant preoccupation with me. My other grave concern was to get some information concerning the whereabouts of my sister, Naomi. I tried to get in touch with refugees who had returned to Oradea-Mare after the defeat of the Germans. I was informed that almost no one had been saved there, because the deportation of the Jews from that city had been carried out with particular cruelty by the Hungarian gendarmerie. Under Hitler, Oradea-Mare, like Cluj, had been returned to Hungary. As this disheartening information was imparted to me, I had to reach the painful conclusion that my beloved sister, Naomi, along with her husband and child, were to be counted among the martyrs of our people. With sorrow I remembered her, a shining example of valorous Jewish women, young, resplendent in her beauty, gentle in her manners. Truly, the words of King Solomon in the Book of Proverbs (31:25), "Strength and dignity were her clothing," were applicable to her. I prayed for her soul, mourned her memory. She had never ceased to be with me in my affection; I have never ceased to include her in my prayers.

Political events were precipitated in Rumania. Vishinsky's long-range plans were coming to fruition. The government of General Radescu, labeled "conservative," was forced to resign because of violent demonstrations and strikes instigated by the Communists. It was replaced by a more liberally oriented regime that included a few Communist members.

It is appropriate to explain at this point that the plan of the Russians concerning the take-over of the countries that they judged to be in their sphere of interest was everywhere the same. First, force out the existing governments, organize new ones, even if they had to allow for honest elections supervised by international teams, provided that the Communists be on the ballots with other parties. Once a single Communist succeeded in being admitted into the cabinet, he would successively eliminate all other members, replacing them with his fellow Communists. A modern Archimedes, he only needed a small corner of the political universe from which he could lift out the rest of the globe. His dynamics were operating according to rigorous laws. They were successfully applied in Hungary and in Czechoslovakia.

Fortunately for me, the Foreign Minister of the new

government was the same George Tatarescu about whom I spoke before, and who I knew would help me leave the country. I had to act in a hurry for there was no doubt in my mind that this new government would be shortly replaced by an all-Communist one, in which case my flight would become impossible.

One day I read in a newspaper an item, reported by the official Rumanian news agency, that a rabbinical convention would be held in New York in the summer of that same year of 1945. This gave me an idea. I hurried to ask for an audience with Tatarescu, in the hope he would make it possible for me to leave Rumania under the pretext of attending the New York convention.

Tatarescu showed himself as benevolent toward me as he had been in the past. As I submitted my request to him, he remarked, "No citizen can obtain a passport until further notice. No one but the diplomats can travel."

Seized by a bold inspiration, I asked, "Sir, would it not be possible to issue a diplomatic passport for me? That convention in New York will be very important in view of the tragic situation of the Jews of Europe. I should really try to attend it."

He seemed to be pleasantly surprised by my request.

"You are right," he said. "It is important. I will give instructions that a diplomatic passport be issued to you. My services will get the visas of the countries which you will have to transit. I will also ask the Russian military command to provide you with an exit visa."

He gave me his hand and added, "Good luck!"

I was impressed with his swift decision. I knew he would keep his word, but I was worried about obtaining the consent of the Russians. Would they allow me to depart? They may judge that there was no sufficient reason for me to do so, that I was not an important person, just a small rabbi. I could only wait and hope.

INTERLUDE IN BUDAPEST

Daily, I inquired at the Foreign Ministry whether there was any answer from the Russians to its request of an exit visa for me. From the face of the official to whom I was referred, from his gesture expressing helplessness, I knew what he was going to say even before he opened his mouth. Daily, I left the building more discouraged, more depressed. It became clear to me that it was useless to hope for any positive attitude from the offices of the Commander of the Bucharest Region of the Russian military.

One day something happened just the same. I received the visit of a gentleman who introduced himself as being closely connected with the Russian authorities in the Rumanian capital. He spoke to me in Yiddish, stated that he was of the Jewish faith. He was informed of the fact that I was in the possession of a diplomatic passport, and that I had applied for an exit visa to be issued by the Russians. He stated his willingness to help me obtain that visa, but he added, that would involve some money.

I was at once on my guard. How did that man find out that I had my visa application pending? He could have been sent to me to lure me into some illegal action for which I could have been arrested. I was aware that people were frequently framed in this manner. I gave him a cautious answer. My petition for a visa was being handled by the Foreign Ministry, and it would be improper on my part to try to move the case by personal action. The man insisted that he was in a position to offer speedy help. I finally told him that he should leave his name and telephone number, and that I would resort to his services if I felt that this would be the thing to do.

That incident frankly scared me. My application for an exit visa—I reasoned—called the attention of all kinds of people to me. I assumed that the Russians were suspicious of anyone who showed that he was anxious to get out of the country. From the recent past of the Hitler era I had learned to fear the nocturnal knock at the door by agents of the secret police, of whatever political label they might be. I felt it more urgent than ever to leave.

I met again the attorney who had been our spokesman before Mr. Vishinsky and told him about my problem.

"Did you say you had a diplomatic passport?" he asked.

"Yes, but what good does it do me if I cannot leave the country?"

"Listen," he said, "why don't you try to secure the help of the Red Cross?"

"How can the Red Cross help me?"

"I know they have Russian translators. They can give you a certificate attesting to the fact that you travel with the consent and approval of the Foreign Ministry to attend an important meeting abroad; they can ask the authorities to assist you in every way."

"Will such a certificate—if I obtain it—help me get an exit visa?"

"No, but it might help you get through the border without it, provided it is written in Russian and has a big stamp on it!" he answered, winking at me significantly.

I thought I understood him. "You think so?"

"I would take a chance on it. What have you got to lose? The worst that can happen to you is to be turned back at the border crossing."

I only halfway believed him; nevertheless, I could in my situation, let no chance go untried. I went to the Rumanian Red Cross, applied for such a certificate; they referred me to the International Red Cross, the proper authority to deliver it.

There it was, the document, in beautiful Cyrillic type. I could not read its contents, but was assured it conformed exactly to my request. In its possession I packed my few belongings, put the letter of the Red Cross into my passport, and boarded the train toward the frontier. We traveled back to Cluj, then through Oradea-Mare, the city which had seen the happiness and misfortune of my sister, Naomi. Reading the name of the station my first impulse was to get off and stay for a few days in Oradea-Mare in order to try to find out something more positive about her fate. The train stopped there for a short period of time, so I had no opportunity to follow up on my impulse. Moreover, I was afraid of not being able to get out of the country if I interrupted my journey. Besides, I had been informed through various sources that very few Jewish families had remained in that city, and that until a few weeks ago, only a small number of deportees had returned there.

The Hungarian frontier appeared soon after Oradea-Mare. The train again came to a halt. Two Russian soldiers came aboard. Without a word, I handed them my passport with the letter written in Russian lying inside. One of them read the document, frowned, looked at me, seemed surprised. He put his hand on my shoulder. I was convinced he was going to arrest me. I looked at his face and it was then my turn to be surprised. The officer was the same one I had met on my first trip from Cluj to Bucharest! He smiled, returned my papers and said to the other soldier: "Chorosho! (OK!)"

They passed me, left the compartment. I thought they must have heard the beating of my heart, the sigh that escaped from my chest. What was the kind of "luck" (this word for the lack of any better) that had sent that officer, a chance acquaintance of a few fleeting hours, to meet me there at the crucial crossing, crossroads of my destiny? Silently, but fervently, with an irresistible urge, I addressed a prayer to God, who had been with me in the forced labor camp, had saved me from death, protected my beloved in a time of universal savagery. My feelings were composed of diverse elements; gratitude for knowing that a superior force was protecting me; strength that I derived from that knowledge; joy to feel really free for the first time since I had left my family, which was still mixed with a lingering fear that something might come up at the last moment that would prevent or delay our reunion.

On the Hungarian side of the border I could consider myself more or less out of danger. The Hungarian guards were awed by my diplomatic passport, by my Russian document, which they did not understand; they saluted and got off the train.

I resolved to stay a few days in Budapest, to inquire into the situation of the surviving Jews and get more information about the circumstances that had preceded the defeat of the Germans and saved the greatest number of the Jews of Budapest.

I knew, of course, that the latter had been concentrated in the so-called Jewish houses. I had also been informed of the efforts of Raoul Wallenberg, officially third secretary of the Swedish legation in Budapest, to save the Jews of the capital by giving them Swedish passports and extending the protection of his country to them; how he had borrowed and rented apartment houses, brought food and medicine to those he had succeeded in removing there, and what desperate other moves he had undertaken to wrest the unfortunate victims from the hands of the German and Hungarian Nazis we shall never know. At present the Germans were gone, and a new regime was installed in the government. What was happening to the Jews who had remained or who were coming back from deportation? No matter how anxious I was to be reunited with my family, I regarded it as my primary duty to know.

My first surprise in Budapest was that people were now eager to proclaim their anti-German sentiment. It sounded as though no one ever had uttered a single word against the Jews, or acquiesced in what the Germans had done against them. I was told how the attitude of the Hungarian authorities toward the Germans had changed, and how public opinion had turned during the last phase of the war. As the military situation of the Germans worsened every day, they demanded ever more energetically that the Hungarians send more troops to the fronts, a minimum of fifty thousand skilled workers to German factories, and an increase in the deliveries of food to Germany. These demands were very slowly and reluctantly satisfied by the Hungarian government; the one concerning the sending of skilled workers could not be satisfied at all. The government cooperated with the Nazis only in the measures directed against the Jews, but dragged its feet in other respects. The deportations had cost Hungary more than two billion pengös, paid out of the confiscated Jewish fortunes. They resulted in a sharp decline in the economy, in the impoverishment of the entire nation. The people who had welcomed the deportations, as long as they could step into the positions or take over the properties formerly held or owned by Jews, slowly came to the realization that the occupying German robbed the country of its vital resources. This realization, together with the opening of a second front by the Allies, stiffened the resistance of the Hungarian authorities concerning the German demands. In addition, reports were received about the enormous losses of the Hungarian troops on the Russian front, even before the beginning of the Russian offensive in June, 1944. The Hungarian soldiers had actually been sent to certain death, since they totally lacked any modern military equipment.

The German propaganda machine continued to boast with the invincible strength of the Wehrmacht, proclaiming the certainty of final victory of Germany, but it was no longer believed. Everyone, except the fanatic pro-Nazis, realized that the Germans were beaten and that Hungary was being dragged down into defeat with them. People wondered what would happen to them and to their nation after the war.

By the end of June, Baky could report to Eichmann that the Hungarian provinces were "judenfrei," meaning that there remained hardly any more Jews outside of Budapest.

At that point President Roosevelt sent an ultimatum to the Sztojay government; stop the deportations, or Budapest would be heavily bombed.

Pressure on the same government was also exerted from elsewhere. The Pope addressed a strong plea to it; the King of Sweden wrote a letter to Horthy deploring the deportations and appealing to the sense of chivalry that had once reigned in the armies of the old Austro-Hungarian monarchy.

The Swiss government in turn launched an appeal to the Hungarian authorities, both in their own name and in the name of the Red Cross that had its seat in Switzerland, to stop the deportations and the persecution of the Jews still remaining in Hungary.

The ultimatum of Roosevelt expired on June 29th. On the 2nd day of July, Budapest was subjected to the heaviest bombing in the entire war.

All these factors, the growing hostility of public opinion to the Germans, the resistance of the government to German demands, a new anti-German atmosphere that was developing in high military circles, the pressure exerted on the government by foreign powers, prompted undersecretaries Endre and Baky, the two fanatic Jew-haters, to accelerate the deportation of Jews from the outskirts of Budapest. At that time the number of Hungarian Jews who had been deported amounted to five hundred eighty thousand.

Baky had a special commando unit set up to begin the deportation of Budapest Jews. On July 7th, the capital was surrounded by troops of the gendarmerie. However, just as the operations of the gendarmes were to start General Lazar, an officer devoted to Regent Horthy, ordered the sirens of the bombing alarm to be sounded in the city. The population was scurrying into shelters; during that time tanks and armored cars occupied the strategic points of the capital. Baky was taken prisoner in his apartment. The gendarmes were sent back to their provinces. Endre and Baky still were allowed to keep their portfolios in the government, but were deprived of the authority to supervise Jewish affairs.

Eichmann, who had reported to his superiors that the liquidation of Hungarian Jewry was only a matter of days (while he still continued his negotiations for the exchange of Jews for war materials), left for Germany to obtain new instructions in view of the worsening situation for the Germans in Hungary There were rumors that Hungary would be declared a German protectorate, like Poland, and its administration taken over by the Germans. The members of the Hungarian government resigned, although their resignation was not made public for the time being.

Prompted by the papal intervention on behalf of the surviving Jews, most of the Catholic priests now began to participate in the movement to save the Jews. The head of the Catholic Church, Cardinal Serédi, who had shown himself an opportunist, unworthy of the example of Catholic prelates in Holland, Norway and France, during the time of the greatest need of the Jews, now ordered that a list be set up of the names of people baptized before 1941. He declared that they were Catholics and as such under the protection of the Church. A few Jews could depart for Palestine thanks to immigration certificates forwarded by the Papal Nuncio, Monsignor Roncelli; still others received safe conducts issued by him.

Protestant bishops also joined in the opposition to the deportation of Jews. Some of them were sheltering people of Jewish faith and helped them disguise their identities, while they urged the authorities to resist the German demands. In fact, resistance to the occupants and their Hungarian stooges was growing everywhere.

Eichmann returned from Germany with an ultimatum;

either the Hungarian government would deport the Jews with maximum speed or he, Eichmann, would have them deported within three days.

This threat had to be taken seriously. Visibly, Eichmann's office made preparations for the deportation.

However, Mr. Bencze, the new Minister of the Interior of the Hungarian government, was not to be intimidated. He conferred the power of decision concerning Jewish matters to his trusted man and confidant, Colonel Ferenci, with the strict order that under no circumstance should he allow the deportation of any further Jewish contingents. Ferenci surrounded the capital with nineteen thousand of his men, ready to engage the Germans in case of a showdown. Eichmann did not dare risk a clash between his soldiers and the Hungarians. He had to give in. The Jews of Budapest were saved once more. It was the first time that the occupying Hitlerites retreated before the opposition of an occupied nation!

Such a situation could not be tolerated. Eichmann regarded the conflict between him and the Hungarian government as a personal challenge. He understood that the Hungarians defied him because they were convinced that Germany had lost the war. He was aware of Horthy's efforts to get in touch with the Allies. He reported this to Berlin, and asked for reinforcements.

It was then that the Wallenberg saga unfolded. Raoul Wallenberg had been sent to Budapest in the capacity of third secretary of the legation there. His real task was, however, to do his utmost to save as many Jews as possible.

He was singularly qualified for this task. Descendant of a long line of statesmen, prelates, military and financial leaders, son of a naval officer, grandson of a diplomat, Raoul Wallenberg traveled extensively in Europe and in the Middle East. For a while he lived in Haifa, Palestine, where he witnessed the plight of refugees from Hitler. A man of great sensitivity, he was deeply committed to his humanitarian assignment. He combined in his person the idealist and the practical man. With funds obtained from the Joint Distribution Committee, he bribed Nazi and Hungarian officials liable to help him. In the name of his government, he issued five thousand passports certifying that the bearers had connections with Sweden and were awaiting emigration there. Later, the number of these passports was increased to ten thousand and more. The owners of the Swedish documents were then moved to houses declared to be under Swedish protection. The Swedish flag flew over these buildings and Wallenberg's friends guarded the entrances. Wallenberg established hospitals, nurseries and soup kitchens, employing thousands of Jews there.

Inspired by Wallenberg's example, the Swiss, the Spanish and the Portuguese governments also established programs for the protection of the Jews.

On October 15, 1944, the Germans moved a Panzer division into Budapest and kidnapped the son of Regent Horthy; on October 17th, they installed a new government, appointing Ferenc Szálasi, head of the fanatically anti-semitic Arrow-Crossist Party, to the post of prime minister. His accession was considered by his followers as the official sanction to loot and kill, especially Jews. The crackling of machine guns could be heard all day on the streets. People locked themselves in their apartments. From time to time trucks loaded with Jewish men, women and children, picked up by drunken soldiers, passed at great speed, headed toward the Danube river. There they were aligned along the shores, shot and their bodies were dumped into the water.

The Arrow-Crossists knew that their days were counted; the Russian armies were closing in on the capital. These desperados, ruffians of the worst type, intoxicated by the power that they had seized in a vacuum of power, were feverishly trying to expedite to the other world as many Jews as they could get hold of. They were accompanied on their bloodthirsty excursions by a former Franciscan monk, the Rev. András Kun. This strange priest participated in the beating and torturing of their helpless victims. Wearing the arrow-cross over his ecclesiastical garments, he blessed the murderers "in the name of Jesus Christ," and ordered them to fire on the unfortunate people who, stripped of their clothes, were facing the guns on the shore of the river.

Raoul Wallenberg versus Szálasi, versus András Kun— this in a nutshell was the situation on those critical days in Budapest. Wallenberg had to outdo himself in order to counter the designs of the sinister forces aligned against him. The Germans ordered, and Szálasi willingly signed, the decree by which thirty thousand Jews had to be marched to Austria in order to work in underground munition factories there. The Austrian border was one hundred forty-four miles away; no food, no blankets against the bitter winter cold were provided for them. Hungarian guards, armed with whips, drove them on. Those who were too weak to march, were shot.

Wallenberg rushed to the scene. Exhibiting documents from various authorities, he snatched two thousand of the marchers from the claws of their torturers, and obtained the return of several other thousands later from Austria. The papal nuncio, Monsignor Rotta, issued hundreds of safe conduct documents which were distributed by the Red Cross among the marchers. Notwithstanding these efforts, so many died on the road that Szálasi had to cancel his order. The Jews, exhausted on their arrival, were of no use to the German munition factories.

Every day the match between Wallenberg and the Arrow-Crossists became more bitter, more dramatic. Risking his own life, he often had to rush to the scene whenever he was informed that a carload of Jewish victims was to be taken by the Arrow-Crossists. It was a miracle that these bandits who respected nothing, refrained from shooting or arresting him.

At last, the Russian armies were at the gates of the capital. The Jews of the city sighed with relief. Marshal

Rodion Malinovsky's troops liberated the international ghetto. Wallenberg declared that he would not return to Sweden before the property of the Jews was restored to them.

On January 17, 1945, a Russian automobile stopped in front of the house at 6 Tátra Street, in which Wallenberg's office was located. Several Russian soldiers alighted, entered the office and asked Wallenberg to accompany them to Debrecen, to Marshall Malinovsky's headquarters. He was to discuss the rehabilitation of Jews with the Marshall.

"I do not know whether I am going as a guest or as a prisoner," Wallenberg said to his fellow workers.

It was the last time he was seen in Hungary.

He was taken by the Russians to Moscow. For years nothing was heard of him. To the pressing, repeated inquiries of the Swedish government, Stalin opposed a categorical denial of any knowledge of his whereabouts. In 1957, after Stalin's death, Foreign Minister Gromyko announced that a document certifying Wallenberg's death of a heart attack was uncovered in the archives of a Moscow prison.

His Swedish compatriots never accepted this explanation. They continued the search for the man who had become a national hero in their country. Against enormous odds, interviewing prisoners of many nationalities, penetrating the secrecy that enveloped this whole affair, they obtained evidence proving that Wallenberg was still alive in 1961, and that he lay in serious condition in a mental hospital. It may be that the Russians had, immediately after his arrival in Moscow, locked him up in an asylum, a practice they are now following with intellectuals who oppose their regime. It also may be that Wallenberg, martyr of a saintly mission, cut off from the outside world, despairing of ever regaining his freedom, lost his mind after many years of captivity.

One may ask, why did the Russians arrest Wallenberg? What did he do to them? What danger did he represent for them?

The answer to these questions is that Stalin was suspicious of everyone who had any contact with any foreign power. Wallenberg was preparing to establish a great organization to help the Jews returning from concentration camps reestablish themselves in the postwar world. After the defeat of Hitler, Stalin desired to extend his domination over the entire Danube Basin. Any activity that could consolidate the influence of foreigners was in the way of his plans. Besides, he might have suspected that Wallenberg was a spy for the Americans. In his diseased brain, the entire world conspired against his personal power. In his entire career there was only one man whose given word he never doubted; that man was Adolf Hitler.

The Jews honor Wallenberg's memory. A street was named after him in Budapest. The Israelite Congregation of Pest expressed to him and the Swedish nation their eternal gratitude for saving one hundred thousand of them.

What Wallenberg did for the Jewish victims of Nazi terror was a testimony to human solidarity. His saga should be told and retold from generation to generation. What he could do singlehandedly was not enough, but he did more than the combined might of the rest of the world accomplished under the circumstances.

I wandered in the streets of Budapest. A bloody chapter of history had occurred there only a few months before. Now that chapter was closed, but my mind kept evoking the tragic, heartrending, revolting, incredible scenes that had animated these very same streets. I was assuming the soul, the mind, even the flesh of each of my unfortunate brothers who had been tortured, humiliated, and put to death in that city. I was driven to the shore of the river where their bodies had been floating; I shed tears. I could not help shedding tears for them. I pieced together their story as I just related it. I heard it from various sources, from people who wanted to ease their conscience; also, and especially from eyewitnesses, namely from the Jews who had survived the storm.

At the time of my short stop in Budapest, I could not

learn anything about the fate of the mission of Joel Brand, who as one remembers it, was sent out by Eichmann to negotiate the blood-for-money agreement. The reports that were shown to me were scarce, confused and contradictory. Only later did the truth come out, partly told by Brand himself, partly by historians.* Brand's mission, as everyone knows, ended in failure, and the Jews of the Hungarian provinces perished almost without exception in the holocaust. In a nutshell, here is what happened to that mission:

On May 23, 1944, Brand arrived in Istanbul and was put in contact with Mr. Steinhardt, ambassador of the United States to Turkey. He told him, as well as the representative of the Jewish Agency for Palestine, about Eichmann's offer to release a hundred thousand Jews for each thousand trucks or other war materials he would receive from the Western Allies. Steinhardt cabled to the State Department, adding the further comment that Eichmann had pledged to use the trucks only on the Eastern front against the Russians.

The American authorities saw in Eichmann's offer an attempt to split the Allies. They feared that the Germans might leak the offer to the Russians. During the entire war the Western powers were mortally afraid of the possibility of Stalin's betrayal and of making a separate peace with the Germans, or of rejoining Hitler's camp.

The State Department also received information about Brand's mission from the British government. It called Eichmann's proposal sheer blackmail, or a political maneuver. According to the British, "This proposal implied the suggestion that we should accept the responsibility for the maintenance of an additional million of persons, which is equivalent to asking the Allies to suspend military operations."

Eichmann had set a deadline of two weeks for Brand

---

*Refer to: Alex Weissberg, *Desperate Mission*. (New York: Criterion Books, 1967), a transcription of the story told by Brand to the author; and Arthur D. Morse, *While Six Million Died* (Random House, New York, 1967), pp. 353-8, 361, 371.

to report to him about the success or failure of his mission. Brand was anxious to meet Moshe Shertok, head of the political department of the universal Zionist Land Organization in Jerusalem, later foreign minister in the Israeli cabinet. He cabled Shertok to meet him in Istanbul, but the British, who did not want Brand's mission to succeed, did not authorize Shertok's trip to Turkey. Brand then decided to attempt a meeting with Shertok in Aleppo, Syria. If that failed, he would continue to Palestine.

Brand was warned that the British would arrest him in Syria, a danger that did not exist in neutral Turkey. In spite of this warning, Brand left for Aleppo and was, indeed, taken into custody by the British. They treated him with courtesy and, in general, allowed him freedom of his movements under their supervision. Meanwhile, Shertok managed to leave Jerusalem and to secure an interview with Brand. Shortly thereafter, the latter was taken to Cairo by the British.

In Washington, the War Refugee Board became suspicious of the continued British imprisonment of Brand. It prevailed upon President Roosevelt to send Ira Hirschmann, founder of the War Refugees Board, to Cairo as his plenipotentiary to arrange a meeting with Brand. The President gave Hirschmann a letter endowing him with presidential authority. He was asked to cable back to the president everything he heard and saw.

Hirschmann flew to Cairo and with great difficulty, in spite of the opposition of the British officials in the Middle East, he managed to meet Brand. The latter told him about the urgency of his mission and of the need to continue the negotiations, even though he was convinced that the Allies would not give the trucks to Eichmann. "While we negotiate, there is a chance for hundreds of thousands to survive."

Hirschmann was impressed by the seriousness of Brand. He cabled to Washington, recommending that Brand be sent back to Hungary with instructions stating that "consideration is being given to the proposals in connection with money and immunity." There should be no mention of trucks.

As he sent his cable, Hirschmann did not know that the United States and Great Britain had already decided to terminate any dealing with Brand or with Eichmann. This decision had been prompted by a veto of the Soviet Union. The U.S. Embassy in Moscow had notified the Soviet government of American plans to explore the Brand proposal in the hope of stalling the Nazi extermination schedule. The Russians had been reassured that the United States would not be fooled by attempts to split the Allies.

On June 19, 1944, Ambassador Harriman relayed the Soviet reaction. It was an absolute "Nyet!" The Soviet government did not consider it permissible or expedient to enter into any negotiations whatsoever with any representative of the German government in the matter referred to by the American Embassy.

This veto of the Russian authorities put an end to Brand's mission. Had he been allowed to continue his negotiations, stalling them to gain time, perhaps many Jewish lives would have been saved. He was kept for months in British custody, blaming himself all the time for the deaths of hundreds of thousands of his Jewish brethren. After the war, he was confronted with Eichmann during the latter's trial in Jerusalem. He died of a heart attack in Germany as he gave an impassioned testimony at the trial of Auschwitz officials.

I wandered in the street of Budapest, accompanied sometimes by people I had known from earlier days. One of them, an old scholar who had been miraculously spared by the murderers, once took me aside and said pointing toward a passerby, "You see that fellow? Last April he wore an Arrow-Cross uniform. He shot a couple in the street, man and wife, as they came out of a grocery store. I saw him myself from inside the housedoor where I was hiding. He had wanted to take them, but they fled; his bullets caught up with them."

I was shocked, hearing the statement of my companion. I could not doubt his words, yet I asked, "How is it possible? Why don't you denounce him?"

My friend shrugged his shoulders. "This is a naive question. He is today a member of the Communist Party. He is not the only one who switched labels. After all, what is the difference for them? They do the same job as before, only they do it undercover for the time being."

"How come the Communists have accepted them? Don't they know about their past?"

"Of course they do. Their past actions denote their experience. The Communists need such people utterly void of scruples to establish their own network of spies. They want to be ready for the day they take over. . ."

His words sounded ominous. There was sadness and resignation in his voice.

However, not everything was sad and depressing for me during those few days. A pleasant surprise awaited me. I retrieved three of my wife's sisters, Rachel, Hanna and Sarah. They had been deported from Hungary to Auschwitz, and survived because they had been assigned to work in German factories. They had been sent to different places and were taken to Bergen Belsen into the forced labor camp. In a clandestine way they learned of the whereabouts of my wife and smuggled a note to her stating they were alive. The Americans liberated them and together, they made the trip back to Budapest.

There they were, emaciated, bearing the apparent signs of their long, terrible hardships. I was appalled by their wan appearance, their sickly pallor, their worn condition. Only their eyes sparkled as they met mine. They were happy to be free again and overjoyed to find one of their close relatives. They told me that their mother had been with them throughout almost their entire ordeal, but was separated from them at the last minute before their liberation. They had been advised of my stay in Budapest by a common acquaintance. They embraced me with great warmth, an effusion of words mixed with sobs. I promised them that I would do everything I could in their behalf once I got to Switzerland. They accompanied me to the railroad station, waved "Good-bye" to me with their handkerchiefs.

I leaned out of the window to get a last glimpse of them, but soon they faded from my view.

The train rushed on. I was called to other preoccupations.

SWITZERLAND AND SWEDEN

I was once more listening to the rhythm of the wheels, that cradled my tired body, soothed and quieted my thoughts. I could still see my three sisters-in-law standing on the platform of the railroad station . . . the streets of Budapest . . . the houses that resounded not so long ago with the lamentations of sufferers, with the cries of anguish of the hunted . . . they, the houses have lost their echos, they were silent as I had looked at them from the outside. The tragedy of recent months was already hushed in the silence of history . . . the river that had witnessed so many horrors was rolling on, oblivious to the crimes or sorrows of men. I was tired, mentally and physically, and I wished I could make my mind a blank.

Houses, fields, telephone wires, warehouses, railroad stations, tools left outside, animals, sounds; the train brought them so close, left them so rapidly behind. The inscriptions on the houses, the language on the signs of stores had changed. I was in Czechoslovakia. Praha (Prague), announced a road sign that had an arrow indicating the direction. Military vehicles, Americans . . . it was so good to see them! Their sight gave me a feeling of freedom, like an electric shock. There still exists freedom in the world, I thought; the horrible danger of the enslavement of mankind by the Nazi hordes has been overcome! Noticing the first American soldiers in the outskirts of Prague, Hitler's defeat became a living reality to me. Knowing something by means of a mental process is not the same as a personal experience that flashes through your mind and establishes the actuality of the event.

I then beheld the Russian army camps at the approaches to the same city. My elation about my and the world's new freedom abated immediately. I had learned enough about the kind of freedom that the Russian army brought to the world during my flight from the slave labor column, during my stay in Rumania, to lose my illusions about it.

In Prague, Americans and Russians were together for the time being. General Patton's army had arrived there first, but the Yalta agreement conceded Czechoslovakia to be in the sphere of interest of the Soviet Union. This agreement is still weighing upon Czechs and Slovaks to this day. Recent history shows that it will not be easy for them to get rid of the yoke....

For some reason, unknown to me, our train was directed to pass through Germany, to criss-cross it before entering Austria. With a great detour and great delay, we arrived in Bregenz, the last Austrian station before the Swiss border.

Both the Austrian and Swiss guards came aboard for routine inspections. The Austrians left and the Swiss examined my papers, and then a new surprise awaited me.

"Your Swiss visa has expired. You cannot pass the border," the inspector said.

I felt my blood rush to my head. I thought I was going to collapse.

"But," I stammered, "I am traveling with a diplomatic passport."

"That is true," the inspector answered, "but you still need a visa to enter Switzerland. Yours had expired . . . you must renew it."

He was courteous but unshakeable. The train was halting only for a short while. I had to pick up my luggage and get off, letting it pass the border. I held my head with my two hands. What am I going to do? I tried to collect myself, regain control of my thoughts.

Who could help me in this emergency? The Embassy of Rumania, I concluded. They could prevail upon the Swiss authorities to let me pass. I called the Rumanian Ambassador, Mr. Franasovici in Berne, explained to him my predicament, and to my great surprise, he knew of me and had heard of my departure from Bucharest. He promised to act in my behalf. I should spend the night in a hotel, and I would be called. He asked me whether I had any money. I told him that the Foreign Ministry in Bucharest had granted me two thousand Swiss francs, and that I still had something left from this sum.

The Ambassador kept his word. The next morning I was called by the stationmaster of Bregenz, who asked me to come as soon as possible. The inspector from the other side of the border was waiting for me.

The new visa was stamped into my passport then and there. I immediately telephoned my family from the border, advising them of my arrival on the next train leaving Bregenz. I had lost one day by this incident, but finally I was inside Switzerland, enroute to Zurich. My odyssey was nearing its end. What my feelings were at this juncture of my life, I cannot tell; anything I would say would sound as mere clichés.

There we were, face to face, my wife with my son, my father and mother, my sister, Esther, and her good husband, at the Zurich station.

We kissed each other's tears off our faces, unable to speak. The women were shaking with sobs, trembling like fearful birds.

We arrived at my sister's apartment and it took some time before we were strong enough to tell each other about our unbelievable experiences. The truth surpassed fiction. Theirs began with the departure for Bergen Belsen, Germany, of the special contingent of Jews, hostages in the "goods for blood" deal worked out by Kastner with the unspeakable Eichmann, in December, 1944. My parents and my wife tried to console each other with the hope of eventual freedom. In Bergen Belsen they were not sent to the extermination camp in which so many of their fellow Jews perished in the same locality; nevertheless, their situation was far from enviable. They were in a state of suspense, as it were, liable to be thrown into the gas chamber in case there arose any difficulty in the negotiations with the Nazis. Meanwhile, they were kept on a starvation diet, and had to stand outside in driving rain, in bitter cold or whatever the weather was during the many roll calls.

My little son had broken out with the measles during their transfer to the camp. Of course, there could be no question of medication of any sort. Nature helped him recover. While in camp my wife gave him some of her own food rations. The fact that she herself did not starve was in itself a miracle. I suspect, though I was not told, that my mother cheated at times, adding part of her own rations to that of her daughter-in-law, to save the latter from complete exhaustion. Thus, from sacrifice to sacrifice, sustaining each other by deeds and words, somehow they managed to survive.

Orders had arrived about September, 1944, to their camp to the effect that part of the contingent was to be released, while the rest would continue to be kept till the deal abroad was concluded. Among the former were included my parents, but not my wife and son. The thought of leaving their grandchild and his mother behind, still in the clutches of their tormentors, while they themselves went free, was unbearable for my old parents. A truly Shakespearean scene took place between them and the commander of the camp. My mother beseeched him to let the young woman and the child leave and allow them, the old people, to remain instead. She knelt before him, embraced his knees, entreating him, crying. The commander declared that he could not accede to their entreaty; he had his instructions. Their departure toward freedom was therefore embittered by their separation from my wife and son. Fortunately, Kastner had succeeded in concluding his negotiations regarding this contingent, and in December, 1944, the last hostages were allowed to leave Bergen Belsen for Switzerland. They had to carry their food, and march miles to the train that was waiting for them, a last act of cruelty on the part of their jailers; this hardship, however, was insignificant in comparison with the feeling of relief which overwhelmed them in those final hours of their captivity.

Upon hearing the story of the tribulations of these beloved souls, and meditating upon my own, on the many miracles that had saved us and brought us together again, a mystical thought occurred to me. The Bible says that the sins of the fathers are visited upon their descendants to the third and fourth generation. I said to myself that the converse must also be true, for the Bible clearly states that the merits of the ancestors secure the blessing of the Lord to their descendants. Certainly, pursuing this reasoning, I personally was not worthy of the obvious and miraculous protection thanks to which I had escaped from the hands of murderers; there must have been intercession on the part of the departed of my ascendance on my behalf. This, I continued, was also true of my wife. Her ancestors, great rabbis and wise humanitarians, revered spirits, must have interceded with the Lord, so that our lives were preserved and dedicated to the preaching of His word for the betterment of mankind. In formulating this thought, I remembered the great Goethe whose Faust is saved from the grasp of the evil spirit by the intercession of Margaret; I also remembered Ibsen, who expressed this same idea of intercession in his play, *Peer Gynt*. And, of course, the words of the Psalmist came upon my lips:

Offer to God the sacrifice of thanksgiving, and
pray thy vows to the Most High—Psalm 50:14.

In that first hour of our reunion I vowed that by my deeds I would make myself worthy of God's special protection that had been manifested to me.

I communicated the results of my meditations to my father. He nodded and said, "The ways of the Lord are impenetrable. It is impossible for us, small human beings, to understand the true meaning of our great tragedy. I feel however, that the Second World War with its horrors, devastations and suffering constituted the punishment for the sins of mankind. As to us Jews, we failed to seize the opportunity to build our own homeland offered to us by the Balfour Declaration. We remained insensible to it, clinging to our comfort in the dispersion rather than abandon it and go pioneering in the Land of Israel. That was our guilt . . . our special guilt, for which we have paid so dearly."

We discussed on this occasion my possible return to Cluj, to replace him as Chief Rabbi, to resume our spiritual leadership over our congregation. I informed him of the realities of the situation; religious life was suppressed under the Communists, religious leaders had to conform to their orders, compromise with them, in fact, become their propagandists. There could be no question of spiritual leadership in the old, traditional sense; there could only be betrayal of that idea. In view of this fact, I told my father, I could do more for Judaism and for religion in general, by being active outside of Rumania. I related once more my encounter with the Russian Jewish officer, who told me that I might not be allowed to exercise my profession there.

I was distressed to see how much the physical and moral suffering, endured by my father during the recent past, had aged him. He was but a shadow of his former self; only his eyes sparkled with their old brilliance; his body had become frail and weak. He told me that he had felt guilty about letting me volunteer for labor service; he had gone through a terrible agony after he had lost track of me. He had said to himself that if I had remained with them in Cluj ghetto, the chances were that I would have been saved with them. Then finally they received the news that I was alive. From that moment on, he was satisfied that my going to the labor camp had been a great experience for me, that it would broaden my horizon, that my suffering had not been in vain. In 1950 my father visited Israel. He died in Zurich, Switzerland, in 1956 and was buried in

Jerusalem. He left three books of his authorship: *Dor Dorim* ("Generation of Generations"), a theological dissertation written before the war; *Sabbath and the Redemption of Israel*, written in German in Switzerland; and another book in Hebrew, entitled *Ekve Hatzon* ("Footsteps of Sheep"), in which he optimistically discussed the future of Israel. I treasure these books that have been my companions to this very day.

The day following my arrival in Zurich I called Ambassador Franasovici to thank him for his help. He invited me to see him in Berne, an invitation I could not decline. At the Rumanian Embassy in the Swiss capital I was cordially received as though I had been a very important person. This was real hospitality offered by someone who expected no advantage of any sort in exchange for his kindness, a hospitality that spoke volumes for the character of the host. I regarded the attention of which I was the object as one given in memory, in honor of the legions of the victims perished in gas chambers, in death marches, shot by implacable guards, of those who had choked to death in airless cattle cars, or died of their wounds inflicted by their executioners. This hospitality was not an act of atonement—it could not be that—only a timid attempt at the reaffirmation of human solidarity. It reminded me of the gesture of my Hungarian friend in Cluj who apologized for the misdeeds of his compatriots. There are always individuals who suffer from suffering inflicted on others; they are the ones for the sake of whom one can forgive mankind.

My visit with the ambassador ended the same way in which my visit with my Hungarian friend had ended. In the same delicate way my host offered me money—a sum of one thousand five hundred Swiss francs—"to tide you over the first weeks in your new emigration." He assured me of his further protection in case of need, and wished me success in whatever I would undertake in behalf of my fellow refugees.

My knowledge of German and French, learned during my studies in Switzerland, enabled me to communicate directly with representatives of the Swiss press. The journalists were eagerly interested in whatever I could report to them about my past adventures, because I was the first survivor from Eastern Europe to reach Switzerland. I also was invited to speak before Jewish groups; I pointed out to them how much the countries visited by the war and the survivors of the concentration camps needed urgent and substantial help.

Tact and caution were my watchwords in moving in my new sphere of activity. Officially I was a guest in transit throughout Switzerland; my residence permit could be revoked any time in case the authorities judged that I abused their hospitality. I was not to agitate for the admission of Jewish refugees; throughout this period the Swiss were disinclined to grant the right of asylum of emigrés, victims of racial persecution. True, a law enacted by the Federal Council protected the native Jews from hostile propaganda, prohibiting public incitement of racial or religious hatred; but the government expressed concern about the danger of foreigners (i.e., Jews) coming over the border in great numbers. Since October, 1938, till the outbreak of the war in 1940, the Germans issued passports to Jewish emigrees stamped with an enormous letter *J* (initial of *Jude*, Jew). Such a humiliating distinction actually originated from Swiss proposals; indeed, the Swiss were anxious to exercise complete control over the flow of refugees into their country. Switzerland should serve only as a country of transit, not of immigration.

Another regulation issued by the Swiss federal police in August, 1942, denied the status of political refugees to persons who "became refugees only on racial grounds, e.g., Jews." This abrogation of the traditional Swiss concept of the right of asylum and the resulting policy of barring the entry of untold numbers of Jews threatened by deportation and death were bitterly opposed by both Swiss Jews and large sections of the non-Jewish population. The effectiveness of this opposition, however, was negligible. Toward the end of the war, the number of Jews who had been permitted to take refuge in Switzerland did not exceed twenty-five thousand. Their needs were provided for primarily by the American Joint Distribution Committee and to some degree by the federal and cantonal governments. Substantial funds were also raised among the local Jewish community, as well as among the general population. Our own group of about seventeen hundred Jews, who in two contingents had entered Switzerland along with another group coming from the camp of Theresienstadt, owed their residence permits primarily to the negotiations conducted by Dr. Kastner, and also to the efforts of Swiss Jews.

It must be said in fairness to Switzerland that since the establishment of the State of Israel, it has been maintaining friendly, even cordial relations with the latter.

In the beginning of December, 1945, I received a letter from the Rumanian Legation of Stockholm. It informed me that a large number of Jewish refugees from Transylvania were streaming to Sweden. The Legation was doing all possible to come to the aid of these refugees, the letter added. The ambassador of Rumania to Sweden at that time was Mr. Duca, son of Gheorge Ion Duca, a former prime minister and head of the Liberal Party, who had been murdered in 1933 by members of the Iron Guard, a pro-German, anti-semitic organization that aimed at the establishment of a regime subservient to Hitler. In 1940 that party did come to power, and went down to defeat with the downfall of its idol. It was in the logic of things that the new Rumanian government sent Duca's son to represent it before a nation that always affirmed its independence both from Hitler and the Soviet Union.

During World War II, the Jews of Sweden were not molested. The Chief Rabbi of Stockholm, Professor Ehrenpreis, was respected as an outstanding representative of liberal theology. In contrast with Switzerland, Sweden showed the greatest willingness to extend its protection to the victims of Nazi persecution. In 1942, about nine hundred Norwegian Jews were admitted to Sweden; and in the next year, the Swedish government not only received about eight thousand Jews and some of their relatives from Denmark, but also an almost equal number of Danes fleeing from German occupation.

The Rumanian envoy in Stockholm further told me in his letter that he had read some of the articles published by the Swiss newspapers concerning my person and my preoccupation with the welfare of the survivors of Nazi concentration camps. He expressed his belief that in Sweden I could be useful to the new immigrants, because I spoke their language and was familiar with their lives prior to their deportation.

I pondered upon the ambassador's letter, and came to the conclusion that indeed, I was more needed in Sweden than I was in Switzerland. What I knew about the Swedish attitude toward the refugees, about public opinion in that country, and the backing by the Swedish authorities of Raoul Wallenberg's heroic activities in Budapest, gave me high hopes that I too would find encouragement there in my efforts to bring material help and spiritual solace to my coreligionists. I therefore asked my family to pack.

The refugees in Sweden were not concentrated in one locality, but scattered all over the country. In their temporary quarters, they were given food, medical help and some money. As soon as they were physically able and medically discharged, they were trained in some trade or some practical occupation. The Jewish organization, ORT, was particularly active in this respect. A large percentage of the refugees were quickly absorbed in the Swedish economy. Nevertheless, there were thousands of those who, bodily or mentally, were still carrying the trauma of their recent ordeal, had lost their families and found themselves alone in a world to which they had difficulty in adjusting. One had therefore to make them feel that one cared for them beyond the mere providing for their material needs. Each of them had a story to tell, and each of the stories was heartrending. To achieve the goal of rehabilitation, it was of vital importance to establish a kosher camp where the Jewish dietary laws were observed and to have regular services to bring about a spark of hope to those refugees who desired to retain their traditional way of life. The kosher camp became an immense influence on the refugees who indicated their desire to be housed therein. The Friday evening services there were impressive; they culminated in collective singing and dancing which was a great booster of the morale of all. I was a frequent visitor for the Sabbath to that camp, leaving my family in Stockholm in order to enhance the religious atmosphere and the feeling of togetherness for which the refugees were craving. It was surprising for me to see how quickly ties of comradeship developed among these unfortunates, how their sense of humor, suppressed by the somber events of their recent tragedy, gushed forth, creating an atmosphere if not of happiness (that was impossible), at least of acceptance of their fate.

After a few months of my stay in Sweden I wrote to my father, described to him the results of my efforts and invited him to visit me to see for himself. He came, traveled with me from one place to another, observed the Sabbath together with the members of the camp, and was quite impressed. He could hardly believe how those people who had suffered so much recently could start life afresh. He and I blessed, united in marriage, several new couples who found each other in their exile. It was a most satisfactory period of my life.

I must relate here an incident that remained indelibly imprinted in my memory. In Stockholm I was confronted with a refugee who had seen his young wife and his two lovely children separated from him and sent to the gas chambers by the infamous Dr. Mengele, the Black Angel of the camp of Auschwitz. With a stab of his thumb he had sent them to their death. The husband and father rushed to join them but the man shouted at him, "You stay!" Mengele ordered him to work and he survived, hoping that by some miracle, his beloved had been spared and that they would be reunited eventually. He survived only to lose all hope, to live in total despair. Meeting him the first time

I found him sullen, oblivious to his environment, sunk in deep melancholy. He would not answer my questions; he hid himself in a corner. I learned his story from others. He was receiving psychiatric treatment that seemed to have no effect whatsoever on him. At first, he did not participate in our common observance of the Sabbath, but would just stand at the door and look and listen. Once I told him that I would arrange to have the Kaddish (Memorial Prayer) recited for his wife and children. I asked him to tell me their Jewish names. He gave no answer, but the following week he handed me a piece of paper upon which he had inscribed their names in Hebrew. I invited him to come to the synagogue to attend the Kaddish prayer in memory of his dear departed. He came, sat in the background, and left after the end of the services. He came again the following week, and our cantor, together with the congregation, recited the Kaddish. The third week he came again, but this time the ice was broken. From the back where he had been sitting, he moved forward and joined in the prayer, while his tears were running down his cheeks. We left together at the end of the services and I held his arm. He said to me, "Thank you, Rabbi!" and again a tear was glistening in his eye. From that time on he was like reawakened to life. He spoke and worked with the others, set the tables, tried to help. Prior to my departure from Sweden, he volunteered to work somewhere and I lost track of him.

"The incident I have just related strengthened in me a thought that I had previously believed to be presumptuous, namely that the reawakening of religious feelings could remedy where psychology or psychiatry fails. I then reversed this thought to conclude that the so-called reevaluation of all values, that equates good and evil, proclaimed by cynics, has created this awful 'mal de siècle' which has left an emptiness in the souls of people difficult to fill. Creative inventions begin in the solitary laboratory of scientists; similarly, destructive ideas germinate in solitary minds to infect a greater and greater segment of mankind."

I could not have been effective in my work without the generous help and cooperation of a very great man, a humanitarian in the noblest sense of the word, the Count Folke Bernadotte. He, like his compatriot Wallenberg, became a martyr to his dedication to the ideal of helping the cause of peace on earth and goodwill among men. At the time of my stay in Sweden he was president of the Swedish Red Cross and it was in this capacity that he received me. From the first moment he offered me his cooperation in my efforts to help the refugees, a cooperation that he continued even after my departure from his country.
   Count Bernadotte was very different from the type of person generally attributed to be the average Swede. Far from being reserved, he was warm-hearted, easy-going. In his company one felt immediately at ease. He told me that he had been informed of the death of many former inmates of Nazi concentration camps after their liberation by the Americans. They died simply because they had been overfed in the hours or days following their newly won liberty; their starved bodies simply could not take the heavy food they had been given. He warned me to be cautious in securing food for the camps; the physical condition of the residents of these camps should always be taken into consideration. I told him that a number of the refugees would not eat the food they were given on religious grounds, and that they were in danger of starving. Count Bernadotte thereupon was instrumental in helping me with the Swedish authorities to establish a kosher camp. We remained in close cooperation till the time of my departure from Sweden which occurred in February, 1948.
   In the years 1947 and 1948, Rumania was transformed into a Communist state. My sponsor, Tatarescu, and all my friends in the Ministry and outside of the government had been replaced by Communists. There was some sort of panic among the refugees. They feared that Sweden, being so close to the Soviet Union, might be taken over by the latter as had been Rumania, Hungary and Czechoslovakia. In the latter country Jan Masaryk, son of the founder, Thomas

Masaryk, was found dead in front of the window of his office building, and the Communists concluded that he had committed suicide; many, however, spoke of foul play. His death coincided with the complete take-over of the levers of command by the Communist Party.

In the beginning of 1948 I received an invitation to occupy the post of a rabbi in a Jewish congregation at Mexico City. The situation in Europe appeared to me somber enough. In Sweden itself the Rumanian Legation was now headed by spokesmen of the new regime; we could not expect from them any help. Rather I was described in Communist circles as conservative, which in their language meant reactionary. Most of my Jewish refugees had by that time left the camps. Many returned to the continent of Europe; others remained and found new homes for themselves. I had once more come to a crossroads in my life, threatened with being farther from my parents and friends in Switzerland and elsewhere. Count Bernadotte assured me that the refugees who still lived in camps would have his attention, and I knew that he would keep his word. My wife concurred with my opinion that having escaped from the Nazis, there was no reason for me to risk an entrapment by the Communists. I accepted the invitation to Mexico, to which country I proceeded via the United States.

It was in this year of 1948 that the State of Israel was born as a result of a resolution by the United Nations. The martyrdom of millions of Jews had not been entirely in vain; after two thousand years of exile in the dispersion, the Jewish people were given back their homeland, Israel. The Arab nations did not accept that resolution and attacked the newborn state. Count Bernadotte was sent out as a special representative of the United Nations to serve as an intermediary between the two feuding camps to bring about a peace between Arabs and Jews. He was assassinated in Jerusalem by terrorists. I mourned the death of this great man and cherish his memory as one cherishes that of a dear friend or a brother. I will never forget him.

AMERICA, LAND OF FREEDOM...
A NATION UNDER GOD

The *Gripsholm,* Sweden's beautiful ocean liner, was approaching the shores of the United States. The passengers hurried on the decks, eager to behold the Statue of Liberty, the symbol known to more people on this earth than any other monument. It leapt into our field of vision, greeted by exclamations of delight.

My wife and I stared at it with inexpressible emotion. I know I risk being accused of using banalities because words have been worn out by too much use or misuse. I wish I could restore to the word "liberty" its original, genuine intellectual and emotional impact. After what we had been through, after having witnessed what the loss of liberty meant to individuals and nations, it is an understatement to say that the sight of that statue had a powerful effect on us. That feminine figure rising above the waves, extending the torch of freedom toward all mankind, defied the doctrine of evil that had been imposed on the enslaved on the other side of the Atlantic. Though we hardly knew any English at the time, we understood the words on the façade of the statue, a quotation from the Bible: "Proclaim liberty throughout the land unto all the inhabitants thereof!" —Leviticus 25:10. In our minds, in our hopes the word "land" encompassed the entire globe. Did I not know that the sons of the United States had recently crossed the oceans to sustain a gigantic fight in the defense of liberty, and that thousands of them lost their lives in that fight?!

My wife was expecting our second child. After long minutes of silence, she said, "I wish my child to be born in this country."

I understood her fully, for I shared her thoughts. To us, wanderers, who bore upon our foreheads the mark of two thousand years of suffering of our people, America appeared as a continent untouched by tyranny, free and young, the defender of human values, the defender of faith.

Upon our landing in New York a group of Jewish refugees who had come from Sweden, also representatives of the Union of Orthodox Rabbis from the United States and Canada, were waiting for me on the pier. My arrival had been announced by the principal Yiddish-language paper in the City.

I was desirous of establishing contact with Jewish leaders and decided to stay in New York for a while.

The refugees I left behind in Sweden were, however, due to the possible abandonment of the kosher camp, on my mind. From my hotel, I sent a telegram to Count Bernadotte inquiring about them. Count Bernadotte answered immediately. I quote his telegram, because it illuminates the character of this extraordinary man. The telegram read as follows:

"Rabbi Glasner, Hotel Wentworth, New York.

As camp in Haelsingmo must be used for Finnish refugees unfortunately impossible postpone action Stop The Jews however will form special unit in the new camp and will get same facilities regarding their religion food etc. as before Stop Hope arrangements satisfactory."

Thus I learned that the camp in which the refugees had been housed before my departure had now been utilized for Finnish people who had fled from the Russian occupation of their country during the desperate war that the little country had waged against its giant neighbor; at the same time I saw in Count Bernadotte's telegram one more proof of his true humanitarianism. It inspired me with a new confidence in mankind, a new confidence in spite of all. I thought that there were at all times a few individuals who actually redeemed the sins of thousands; thanks to them, civilization is preserved. In Bernadotte's case, he gave his life for his active love of mankind, just as his compatriot, Wallenberg, would do in the years that followed.

In New York a real surprise awaited me. I received an invitation from King Michael of Rumania to pay him a visit in his quarters at the Waldorf-Astoria Hotel.

The King had arrived in New York at about the same time as I did. How did he happen to think of me? I reflected later upon this question and could come up with only one explanation, even though it appeared at first presumptuous on my part. Rumania capitulated in the summer of 1944, and from then on the Rumanian Army fought on the side of the Allies. In December, 1947, the Communist Party, led by Anna Pauker, demanded the abdication of the King. King Michael was very popular and there were manifestations on the streets of several cities, clamoring his support. The demonstrators were dispersed by Communist soldiers arriving in army trucks. King Michael was forced to quit even though he had received from Stalin in 1944, the medal of the Order of Victory, the highest Soviet decoration, after he had overthrown the regime of General Antonescu. On that occasion, Radio Moscow broadcast a long commentary to praise the King. "This distinction," Radio Moscow said, speaking of the Stalin medal, "symbolizes the courage shown by him when he took his country out of Hitler's war."

President Truman also recognized the courageous action of King Michael, and presented him with the medal of the "Legion of Merit," with the following words:

> By his judgment full of wisdom, by the boldness of his action and by the high example of his personal

conduct King Michael made an invaluable contribution to the cause of liberty and democracy.

In September, 1945, when I arrived in Zurich, I was asked by the representatives of the press what I thought of King Michael. I told them that thanks to him, Rumania was the only exception among the countries subdued by Hitler that dared to oppose Hitler's plan of mass deportation and extermination of the Jews. I insisted on the fact that the Jews of the entire world owed a debt of gratitude to the King and to the Rumanian nation, and that the King's courageous action would be acknowledged by history.

The Swiss press, both the German and French-language press, published these three testimonies in favor of the King. One of them added an anecdote that attempted to illustrate the servility of the Rumanian Communists toward the whims of their masters in Moscow. It goes as follows: Anna Pauker walked one day of bright sunshine in a street of Bucharest, holding an open umbrella over her head. She was accosted by a passer-by who told her, "Your Excellency, why that umbrella? We have beautiful sunny weather." Anna Pauker replied in a dignified tone, "Comrade, it is raining in Moscow!"

Anna Pauker obeyed the wish of Moscow when she forced the abdication of the King. King Michael was given a safe-conduct to leave the country and Rumania was proclaimed a "People's Republic."

King Michael received me in a very friendly way, and expressed his appreciation for my humanitarian work, commended me on my efforts on behalf of the refugees. I, in turn, thanked him for his protection of the persecuted Jews, for preventing mass deportation and for bringing back those thousands who had survived the camps.

Aside from the King, I also had the opportunity of meeting Mr. Gafencu, a former foreign minister, General Radescu, who headed the Rumanian government at the time of my stay in Bucharest, and Mr. Vishoianu, former foreign minister of Rumania. All these men, who not so long ago played an eminent role in the shaping of history, were now refugees like myself. This thought constituted a lesson for me about the instability of human fate and fortunes.

I pondered a great deal during those first days on the soil of America about the direction my further activities should take. I was supposed to take up my post in Mexico City, but the Jewish leaders of New York repeatedly expressed to me their opinion that I would meet with more challenge in the United States than in a relatively isolated position in Mexico. I was ignorant both of the English and of the Spanish language; wherever I settled down I would have to learn the language of the country, for I could not see myself unable to communicate with people in their native tongue.

It was necessary, I decided, to make the trip to Mexico, just to see and make a comparison. Our journey there turned out to be most inauspicious. My wife came down with a serious dysentery; I was in great anxiety for her and the unborn child. The congregation that had invited me was a traditional orthodox congregation. The Mexican Jews in their majority had long been established in the country; there were few refugees among them. I remembered that it was explained to me that in Chinese writing the ideogram of challenge was represented by crisis and danger. By my past, I was preconditioned to challenge and was too young to settle down in a relatively established position with little opportunity for growth. It became obvious to me that I would reach a much larger audience if I preached and taught in English.

At last my wife recovered and we returned to the United States where my wife gave birth to our second son, David. Thus her wish, expressed at the sight of the Statue of Liberty, was fulfilled. I began to learn English with great enthusiasm. It did not take me very long before I could understand and grasp fully the meaning of the preamble to the Constitution: "We, the people of the United

States, in order to form a more perfect Union, establish justice ,insure domestic tranquility, provide for the common defense, promote the general welfare, and secure the blessings of liberty for ourselves and our posterity, do ordain and establish this Constitution for the United States of America."

I wonder whether the generations born under the protection of this inspiring document are so penetrated by its wisdom and appreciate its intent to the same extent as we, newcomers to the country did.

Presumably the Statue of Liberty, greeting countless immigrants upon their arrival in the United States, gave them the same joy it gave us, the same courage to start a new life. It was this notion of living in a free land that inspired subsequent generations to make this nation great.

For us, the document represented a benevolent law, civilization, encouragement to do well for one's self and for others. I was truly grateful to have been allowed to be here, to have my newborn son become a citizen of the country by the mere fact of his birth on American soil.

At the end of 1948, while I was in New York City, I was appointed director of the Synagogue Council of Mizrachi, National Religious Zionist Movement. Soon I was solicited for numerous speaking engagements. In 1949, I established my own synagogue on Central Park West, in New York. Unfortunately, the climate of New York and of the East Coast was not good for me. I also developed a serious allergy which was undermining my health. On the advice of doctors, with great regret, I had to leave for more clement skies. In 1952 we moved to California.

I regretted leaving New York, but had no cause to regret my establishment in California. Throughout all these years I never lacked the opportunity to serve ideals dear to me. The conviction of being useful had made me happy; it encourages me to continue as long as I am able to do so. The present endeavor of writing the story of my life is part of my overall efforts to serve my fellowmen.

The upheavals in the sixties, the burning of cities, the demonstrations, bombings, filled me with great sorrow. I heard the new slogan echoing through the air: "God is dead!" For me there was direct relationship between the violence in the streets and the loss of faith that this slogan indicated. Deprived of it, the young staggered without any moral support through life. They had nothing to hold on to; angry, frustrated, they vented their frustrations on inanimate objects like angry men often do.

In those days of crisis when people questioned the very survival of American civilization I happened on Aldous Huxley's novel, *Point Counterpoint*. Leafing through it, I was attracted by the following dialogue:

> "I simply cannot believe [says the woman protagonist] that thick arteries [meaning old age] will ever make me believe in God and Morals and all the rest of it. I came out of the chrysalis during the war, when the bottom had been knocked out of everything. I don't see how our grandchildren could possibly knock it out any more thoroughly than it was knocked then." "They might have to put the bottom in again," suggested Spandrell [her male partner].

By mere chance—or was it?—I came upon this passage in the book and I cannot describe how much it galvanized me. The Second World War like the first one was a period during which the bottom had been knocked out of everything, and it was important, imperative that we should help put it in again!

I became the rabbi of the Congregation of Beth Abraham in City Terrace, in Los Angeles. I joined the Eagud Harobonim, the Alliance of Orthodox Rabbis; later I was elected vice-president of the Orthodox Rabbinate of Greater Los Angeles, vice-president of Christians and Jews for Law and Morality, chairman of the Interfaith Committee of Los Angeles for Released Time for Religious Instruction. In addition, I am a member of the Mayor's Community Advisory Committee, the District Attorney's Advisory Council, and a member advisor for the committee of the state Attorney General's office. My time was pretty well filled up, yet I remained unsatisfied for I wished to give more of myself, to communicate my beliefs based upon my past experience to large audiences.

I regarded it as a great opportunity to serve when I was called upon to testify in the matter of the Dirksen Constitutional Amendment to permit nondenominational voluntary prayer in public schools. For some strange reason, a number of clergymen of various denominations opposed that amendment. On August 4, 1966, I went to Washington and made an appeal for its passage.

In essence, I argued, the atrocities to which millions of innocent people were subjected during World War II and to which many are subjected in the far-flung corners of the world today were caused, and are caused, by the totalitarian states which deny the existence of a Creator and Supreme Being. From my study and meditation on the tragedies I witnessed, I have come to one conclusion, namely, that not considering themselves accountable to a Supreme Creator, the leaders of these countries believe themselves above moral laws and thus become destructive to life.

Standing before the congressional committee I pointed out that the interpretation of the U.S. Supreme Court which forbade a voluntary (I emphasized the word "voluntary") nondenominational prayer in schools on the ground of the freedom of conscience stipulated in the First Amendment, ignored the living fact that not only our Founding Fathers, but most of our citizens, had in mind a nation relying upon divine providence.

I expressed the opinion that human relations based upon the notion of a higher destiny of man, the respect of spiritual values, alone offered a solid foundation for the future of our country; they were more important than the stress of technicalities. Depriving children of their right to say a prayer before they started their daily work robbed them of hope and reliance upon a benevolent force that assured to them a purpose in life and the tranquility of their minds. These values prevalent in schools reflected inevitably on the homes. The converse was also true; their absence was disturbing both for the children and their parents.

Indeed, I said, there were millions of people throughout the nation who were deeply affected by the decision of the Supreme Court prohibiting the mention of God.

The essence of wisdom consists of recognizing that man's free will is his most precious possession. It enables him even to disassociate himself, if he so chooses, from his Creator to whom he owes this gift. No individual or group of individuals should have the right to deprive man of this unique privilege. Man should be free to seek and praise and serve, or even to ignore, his Creator in his own way, so long as he does not interfere with the next person's equal right. The Founding Fathers understood and gave attention to this concept when they provided that men as a group, through their government, should make no law respecting the establishment of religion. Religion, in its simplest form, is the formal worship of a Supreme Being. The Founding Fathers thereby separated church and state.

But if our forefathers were quick to express the principle of separation of church and state in the Constitution, they were also quick to affirm that the powers of the federal government were delegated from the "reserve" held by the people. Previously these same Founders, in the Declaration of Independence, had held it to be self-evident that the people are endowed with a reserve of certain inalienable rights which were bestowed upon them by a Supreme Being. In short, while the Founders were loathe to impose upon man's freedom of conscience where religion was concerned, they were quick to acknowledge their own, and this country's dependence upon a Supreme Being. They did not purport to separate God and state, but only the church and state. To some, the distinction may seem subtle, but the distinction is nevertheless there.

It appears that our Founding Fathers were equally concerned when they wrote the Declaration of Independence based on the biblical premise that all men are created equal—not to infringe on the rights of any denomination. If the Declaration of Independence is valid, then a voluntary nondenominational prayer is just as valid and not in conflict with our Constitution. Our Founding Fathers felt the state should not tell man how he is to worship his Creator, or that he should worship, if he does not recognize a Creator. However, the state, so long as the majority wishes, should acknowledge its dependency upon a Supreme Being. This was done through official emblems, slogans, oaths, declarations and speeches, and official holidays. The Founders did this because history had taught them that the nation which respects a Supreme Being enjoys divine protection and blessing. How right they were has already been demonstrated. On the other hand, nations which refused to honor, respect or even acknowledge a Supreme Being met with ultimate destruction.

The conflict today is not between one religion or another, but between those who believe in the existence of God and those who do not. The latter (who at this time are in the minority) claim that their conscience is offended by the very mention of a Supreme Being in public, even though they are free to abstain from mentioning Him.

I further submitted to the consideration of the senators, that the Preamble of the Constitution was equally as important and valid as the First Amendment. It was up to the Congress of the United States to bring about clarification of the First Amendment so that those who desire to recite a nondenominational prayer may do so under the law and not be prohibited, for such prohibition is as much a denial of the individual's right to believe and to pray as would be the imposition of prayer on nonbelievers. I said that in my opinion one of the greatest educational tools is lost when we do not tell our children that those who desire to pray to Almighty God may do so, and those who do not believe in prayer may abstain. This concept, I maintained, was the cornerstone and pillar of our American way of life, namely, to differ and remain together united in the brotherhood of man. For all these reasons, I said, I believed that the proposed Dirksen Amendment was needed, and if Congress would not enact it we would find ourselves to be in conflict with our traditions.

The amendment did not pass, but my testimony was not without effect. Newswire services carried excerpts of my testimony, and some major newspapers such as the Chicago Tribune printed it in its entirety. The late Senator Everett Dirksen praised my testimony as he was interviewed on "Meet the Press" on NBC.

Another statement before the California Senate Educational Committee was presented by me when the question of sex education in schools was considered. There was an amendment to sex education legislation added to the original bill which provided that only those children in public schools whose parents gave written request should be exposed to sex education. I was prompted to speak about this subject because of what I had seen and observed during my stay in Sweden. In that country, sex education was supported by the government for more than twenty years, and was made compulsory for all school grades for ten years. Irrefutable statistics coming from diverse research sources concurred to the effect that almost 90% of Sweden's inhabitants had premarital relations before they reached their twenties. Contraception is in Sweden a compulsory subject for youngsters fourteen years and over, and they also receive instruction in venereal disease prevention, because of its enormous burden to the country. In spite of the foregoing facts, Sweden has one of the highest rates of venereal disease in addition to the rates of suicide and alcoholism, and nowadays also of drug addiction.

To the Senate Education Committee I submitted the

above facts and added that here again, as in many other areas, the state, by adopting this program, would usurp the right and duty of the parents to enlighten their children. Sex education requires an individual approach; how much and what should be told to the child cannot be given uniformly in the classroom. Sex education as proposed in the present form would therefore not be beneficial to our young students.

The conditions, I further said, prevalent in Sweden were sufficiently proving that we were treading on dangerous grounds. To embark on such a questionable program was highly risky. After all, we, of the older generations, reached maturity without all these new methods. Let us rely on our past experience and not venture to experiment with innovations which may damage and intoxicate our youngsters' minds beyond repair.

I knew that my testimonies regarding the prayer amendment and sex education would bring upon my head the hostility of a great number of people, that I would be called old-fashioned and reactionary, but I could not and would not keep silent because my faith and my life experience commanded me to speak up.

Such questions important to the larger human community naturally challenged my will to stand up in the defense of my opinions. Meanwhile, my duties as an Orthodox rabbi required my day-to-day attention. One of the tasks I considered primary throughout my entire life was to see to it that my coreligionists who desired to observe the dietary law of their religion should be enabled to do so.

Soon after my arrival in California, I became aware of the fact that this state lacked an enforcement agency of the State Kosher Food Law that prohibits the sale of food products fraudulently termed "kosher," not prepared according to Orthodox Hebrew religious requirements. I vividly remembered the anguish in Sweden of the refugees who would rather starve than eat non-kosher food; this was the reason which prompted me to be interested in this question. In my opinion it was not only morally wrong, but was also liable to cause deep emotional disturbance to Orthodox Jews who would have discovered that they were defrauded in buying supposedly kosher products. Accordingly, together with my colleagues, we turned to the leading legislators to seek legislation that the State Kosher Food Law (Penal Code 383 B) should provide for enforcement.

The then-governor, Goodwin Knight, heeded our request, supported by the Joint Legislative Budget Committee, in that they authorized the Department of Finance to conduct a survey throughout the state to ascertain the extent of violations of the State Kosher Food Law. Two rabbis and myself were appointed to conduct the survey and to report back to the legislature of the results of the study. Our investigation revealed flagrant violations of the law. Based on our report, in January, 1957, Assemblyman Joe Shell introduced legislation to provide enforcement of the "Kosher" state laws. We recommended that an item be included in the 1957 state budget for the establishment of proper enforcement to be supervised by an Orthodox rabbi. In view of my experience, this task of supervision was assigned to me. I was appointed Kosher Food Law Representative.

These various activities carried me through the years, from my arrival in California in 1952 to the year 1968. In that year a new opportunity arose for me to fulfill my ideal of "putting back in the bottom that had been knocked out of everything," to use the language of Aldous Huxley.

In 1968, I started a series of television talks in connection with the Jewish holidays with a view of stressing the importance of faith in our lives. I could not think of anything that would have made me happier than this opportunity to spread God's word. Later, I also had a regular weekly radio talk on the program called "Time for the Truth."

Thinking out my assignment I concluded that my talks

should introduce Jewish customs, acquaint the viewer with Jewish ethics, but that they should transcend these topics and touch also upon problems interesting everyone. I began, I believe, in February, 1968, with the interpretation of the meaning of the Passover festival in the life of the Jews. I started with this subject because the Passover holiday commemorates the deliverance of the Jewish people from Egyptian slavery; by extrapolation it referred to our and the world's present situation. World War II saved the peoples enslaved by Hitler; the Passover does, however, not only commemorate the past—it is also filled with hope concerning the future. I wished to bring a message of hope for a brighter future, namely that freedom will ultimately come to all. I would have liked to impart to my listeners a deeper understanding of the real character and intentions of the leaders of the world-wide revolutionary movement, the menace that emerged after the defeat of the Hitlerian conspiracy, which has not removed tyranny from this earth.

The radio program "Time for the Truth" had for its leit-motif: Return to God! Patiently, strong in our faith, we would have to restore the belief in the divine mission of man that two world wars had all but extinguished in the souls of the young generation. I was able to point out a significant fact. In our country religious affiliation dropped from 49% in 1958 to 44% in 1966; in the Soviet Union—the latest surveys indicated—half a century of extensive anti-religious propaganda still left 28% believers of the total population. Also that in Poland and in Hungary church services were attended by people of all ages and of all walks of life.

"It is obvious," I commented, "that there is a connection between America's religious decline and America's present social and moral upheavals."

Was this not the time to quote the Bible: "And many evils and troubles shall come upon them; so that they will say in that day: Are not these evils come upon us because our God is not among us?"—Deuteronomy 31:17.

I spoke to my audience about suffering, attempted to respond to the baffling and ever-recurrent questions of why suffering exists and why God allows the good to suffer and the wicked often lead an apparently happy life. These questions have been debated by innumerable people, laymen and religious, and the answers are as numerous as are those who spoke to the subject. Sifting the arguments that come to my mind, I finally stop at one and give it to you. My answer is this: suffering is man-made for the most part. The majority of the evils that beset humanity, the wars, poverty, the insecurity of life, alienation, tortures, starvation, and many other calamities are brought about on humans by their fellow humans. They far outnumber the natural disasters, such as earthquakes, tornados, floods, fires, or the natural exhaustion of the body with advanced age. Man has a choice: he can create either paradise or hell on earth, and whatever he does, he is responsible. It has been given to him to combat or eliminate diseases; he can slow down the decay of the body; he must bear the responsibility for the society he lives in. It is by its fruit that you know the tree; it is by the result of his action that man should be judged. Free choice and freedom are interrelated, for freedom without free choice makes no sense. Man is free because he can choose between good and evil; a society is free when it allows free choice to the citizens. God created man free and responsible. It should be the same with a society and its citizens. In a totalitarian society the citizens do not make decisions concerning the running of the state; only the leaders do. The freedom of decision has been taken away from the citizens; they are not responsible. They are responsible only for allowing a totalitarian society to be created and for tolerating such a society, and they must bear the consequences of their indifference in this regard.

The more I preached the more I felt the need for action in this age of mounting and recurrent crisis. I received encouraging letters praising me far beyond my merit. I received many commendations on my television talk given on the eve of the Jewish High Holidays; among others, one stated that my message and the accompanying cantorial and choir chanting were profoundly inspiring and truly uplifting, and that "such inspiration must live so long as memory lasts." I was not insensible to such encouragements; they spurred me on to continue on the path I had traced out for myself.

I must add, for the better understanding of my position as a rabbi and an American citizen, that I have never disassociated in my mind my services to Judaism and those I owe to America. For me the two remain inseparable; I conceive and interpret literally the words "One nation under God" as binding for me. Serving God, I serve the nation. My congregation, Mishkan Yicheskel sponsored, starting in 1965, an annual God and Country Award. Every year we honor persons who by their deeds have distinguished themselves in proving their dedication to the American ideals of freedom and opportunity, those who fearlessly cherish and perpetuate the principles handed down to us by our Founding Fathers. In 1969, we counted among our honorees Justice R. S. Thompson; Mr. Harry Von Zell, noted television and radio personality, Honorary Mayor of Encino, California, who spent many years of effort to upgrade standards of morality in the entertainment field; James E. Johnson, a twenty-one-year career officer in the Marine Corps; Don Belding, who had prominent leadership posts in Freedoms Foundations, The Arthritis Foundation, Easter Seal Society, and Crippled Children's Society; Bernard Spiegel, a leading figure in the Orthodox Jewish community who was also a recipient of the God and Country Award. In 1970, our honorees were Associate Justice Marshall F. McComb, of the California Supreme Court; Albert Collins, a key figure in the Food Industry for America, an organization to promote patriotism and an appreciation of our American heritage and the free enterprise system; Sam Campbell, the well-known editor of the

Anaheim Bulletin; Lawrence Welk, who has been known as the "Champagne Orchestra" man to two generations of Americans. Among other honorees of the past I cannot omit George Putnam, the eminent television broadcaster; Mr. and Mrs. Patrick J. Frawley, Jr., prominent civic and philanthropic community leaders; and Dr. Vierling Kersey, well-known educator and civic leader. At our sixth annual God and Country Awards Dinner, held in the Palladium Ballroom in Hollywood, with Secretary of Transportation John A. Volpe as principal speaker, the list of persons present read like the "Who's Who" of the supporters of the American creed. Associate Justice McComb expressed his belief to the assembled guests stating, "How fortunate you and I are to believe in God and our wonderful nation. I shall always remember this inspiring event."

I mention all the above, not to boast about what I have done since I have become an American, but to point out that much can be and must be done to stand up to the challenges of our days. Arnold Toynbee, the illustrious historian, said, "A civilization survives or becomes extinct depending upon the success which it achieves in living up to the challenges that confront it." Is it necessary to insist that no civilization can live up to the challenges that confront it without being animated by a religious spirit? Religious spirit in whatever form constitutes the greatest force of every individual and of every nation. It overcomes the most sophisticated weapons of modern technology, just as it overcomes every obstacle that bars the path to spiritual growth of the individual. Paradoxical though this sounds, historical examples abound to prove it.

THE INVINCIBLE WEAPON OF FAITH

> Not by might, nor by power, but by my spirit, saith the Lord of hosts—Zechariah 4:6.

I have related in the previous chapters how prayer and faith gave me the force to resist despair and to make split-second decisions that saved me from certain death. Recent stories told by others confirm the fact that people who had faith in themselves, in Providence, in the higher destiny of man, survived the most horrible tortures, suffering inflicted by their enemies aimed at breaking not merely their bodies, but above all their spirits.

The prisoners of war returned from North Vietnam attested to the power of faith and prayer under immense distress. President Nixon, in his March 29, 1973, message to the nation, reported the following day by the *Los Angeles Times*, said:

> A few days ago, in this room, I talked to a man who had spent almost eight years in a Communist prison cell in North Vietnam. For over four years he was in solitary confinement. He never saw another person except his captors in that time. He lived on two meals a day, usually just a piece of bread and a vegetable soup. All he was given to read was Communist propaganda. All he could hear on the radio was Communist propaganda.

I asked him how he was able to survive it and come home standing tall and proud, saluting the American flag. He paused a long time before he answered. Then he said, "It isn't easy for me to answer. I am not good at words, but all I can say is that it was faith—faith in God and faith in my country."

The *U. S. News & World Report,* in the May 14, 1973 issue, reports an interview with John S. McCain III, Lieutenant Commander, U. S. Navy. In his story he reveals that prayer sustained him in time of trial. He continued, "I was finding that prayer helped. It wasn't a question of asking for superhuman strength or for God to strike the North Vietnamese dead. I was asking for moral and physical courage, for guidance and wisdom to do the right thing. I asked for comfort when I was in pain and sometimes I received relief. I was sustained in many times of trial."

Even when the forces of evil capture and crush the body, the spirit of men can be free. To return to events during World War II, facts were related to us that fill me with humility and pride at the same time: humility because I realize how much we all need to strengthen our spirit; pride in knowing that some of my fellow Jews retained their faith in spite of the degrading efforts of their enemies. Let me select a few of the many examples of the triumph of strong belief in God and in man's spiritual nature over the destructive forces of unbelief.

Humans were herded in cattle cars, on their way to extermination. The rhythm of the wheels mixed with the wails and screams of the victims; despair, gloom, hopelessness everywhere, a cacophony of laments, a lamentable final chapter of human existences. Suddenly there was a hush, then a different concert, a melody arose above the sobs and screams. It was hummed at first in a minor key, then it was joined by many voices to change into an anthem of hope and triumph. Arms were locked, a ring was formed. Shadows began to sway, then to move and finally to dance and sing.

This was the dance of the doomed, the ballet of the dying. What were they saying? What was the strange lyric of this fantastic song? It was the unextinguishable faith: "I believe in perfect faith in the coming of the Messiah."

The word "Messiah" might be understood literally, as did those who sang that hymn; it also might be conceived in a figurative sense, as the symbol of a better future for man. It is this "perfect faith in the coming of the Messiah" which is the indispensable element of the building of such a better future; it is the positive element which must and will rise if mankind is to be saved from destruction.

In April, 1944, the well-known Rabbi Sholom Eliezer Halberstam, of blessed memory was brought to the Nyiregyháza ghetto in Hungary along with other victims of Endre and Baky. He was at that time eighty-two years old; his wife, eighty-five, also taken to the ghetto, died there before his eyes. A few days later the deportees were as usual herded into cattle cars that were sealed and departed toward their sinister destination.

In Auschwitz the son of the old rabbi was shot by an SS officer who knew why he used up a bullet on a deportee who could have been sent to the gas chamber. He had learned about the identity of the rabbi and his son; he was a sadist desirous of inflicting superhuman suffering on the Jewish leader. With the corpse of his son lying before the old man, he was asked by the Nazi officer, "Where is your God to whom you always pray? Why did he not save your son? Why does he not save your people? Do you still believe in Him?"

The rabbi's answer was reported by three survivors of the camps. It was as follows: "I firmly, unwaveringly, believe in Divine Providence."

These were his last words. The Nazi officer, grinning, but angry and embarrassed, pointed with his thumb to the left, which meant that the old rabbi had to be dragged to the gas chamber.

Grand Rabbi Joseph Weiss of Spinke, a resident of

Szölös, Hungary, sheltered refugees as long as he was able to. On April 16, 1944, he himself, along with the other Jewish residents of his community and of the nearby villages, was taken to the ghetto to be deported. The deportation from Szölös to Auschwitz was carried out in three different groups. The rabbi was in the last group that left on May 23rd. In the sealed cattle car, fully aware of the fact that they were being taken to their death, the rabbi entuned the song: "Oh Lord, purify our hearts that we may serve Thee truthfully." The other deportees sang with him. The faith of the rabbi enabled them to overcome their fear of dying; their bodies were doomed, but their spirit was victorious. Indeed, faith triumphed in that case over death.

The last words of this great man were taken from Leviticus 6:5—"Fire shall be kept burning upon the altar continually, it shall not go out."

The Jewish people have a two-thousand-year history of dispersion and persecution during which they have been living by their faith. In their everlasting struggle they were nurtured by the unending belief in one invisible, but everpresent God. This made them together with the Christians, special targets of the Romans, who were accustomed to carve out their divinities in stone and wood, and who feared this unknown God. The Judeo-Christian culture which formed the Western world since the collapse of the Roman Empire, has ever since remained the special target of the tyrants. Indeed, as long as this Judeo-Christian culture survives, the dignity of man will be upheld; there can be no lasting tyranny as long as the belief in man's spiritual destiny is still alive. Hitler focused his destructive power on the Jews as primary targets because they were helpless, but he aimed at the same time at all Christians, and in fact, at the dignity of man. His rage against all believers was irreducible. Deep down he knew, as the Communists know, that faith can never be extinguished in the hearts of human beings, for what characterizes us is our thirst for transcendence. Without faith man remains but an animal, who eats, lives, reproduces his species and dies.

In the history of our times there are chapters that have brought new insight into the power of faith as a weapon to be used in critical times of a nation's history. One of these chapters is the fight for the independence of India under the leadership of Ghandi, a frail man who wore hardly any clothes, let alone any murderish weapons. He invented the method of nonviolent resistance to the British who found it impossible to combat and had to give up finally. Ghandi preached that man is precious and that it is wrong to oppose one's foes with the power of weapons. He opposed them with the power of words that proclaimed his deep belief in the sanctity of the spirit. He taught that it was possible to resist wrong by not complying with the dictates of the oppressors, taking the risk of retaliation by the latter. He succeeded in convincing hundreds of millions of his people. The power he created consisted solely of the faith in the justness of their cause; this power proved to be more potent than prisons, tanks, machine guns or bombs dropped from airplanes. After Ghandi the people of India no longer exhibit this unity that was theirs during his lifetime, but the power of faith has been demonstrated and it is certain that it will be used victoriously again whenever the masses share a common belief, a common ideal temporarily suppressed by force.

One can say without exaggeration that the British themselves owed their victory over Hitler's Luftwaffe to the faith with which they were inspired under their God-sent leader, Winston Churchill. At a time when Hitler was at the peak of his power, when he boasted that he would erase England from the map, when Poland was dismembered, France lay prostrate and England remained alone to fight him, Churchill stood up and told his compatriots and the rest of the free world not to despair, not to lose faith. Churchill, who was then in his seventies, represented in those depressing days faith in man as bearer of the divine spark, as opposed to man reduced to the level of animals, malleable at will. He promised to his country nothing but blood, sweat and tears in the near future; he announced that the defenders of freedom would fight from the hills and the valleys, on the sea and on the land till final victory. The two fingers of his right hand extended in the form of a V became the symbol of hope not only in England, but in all countries temporarily trodden by Nazi boots. His words broadcast over clandestine radios, translated into several languages, rekindled the spark of resistance. His enemies feared and tremendously respected him. The V of Churchill's fingers proved to be much stronger than the V of the German "Vergeltungswaffen," the rockets they launched at defenseless populations across the Channel.

Churchill's inspiring words became as famous as Lincoln's Gettysburg address. He said:

We shall not flag or fail; we shall go on to the end. We shall fight in France, we shall fight on the seas and oceans, we shall fight with growing confidence and growing strength in the air; we shall defend our island whatever the cost may be, we shall fight on the landing grounds, we shall fight in the fields and in streets, we shall fight in the hills, we shall never surrender, and even if, which I do not for a moment believe, this island or a large part of it is subjugated and starving, then our Empire beyond the seas, armed and guarded by the British Fleet would carry on the struggle until, in God's time the new world, with all its powers and might steps forth to the rescue and liberation of the old.

The new world with all its power and might did step forth to the rescue and liberation of the old because a man in a wheelchair shared Churchill's faith. President Roosevelt essentially repeated Churchill's words when he proclaimed in one of his historic speeches that "We have nothing to fear but fear itself." Those who studied the methods employed by the Nazis to subjugate foreign peoples, know that they tried first of all to strike terror into the hearts of the latter to weaken their resistance. Roosevelt's words were no mere rhetoric: they were realistic, statesmanslike. Fear is the opposite of faith; fear is destructive, faith is constructive.

The history of the American nation is indissolubly connected with the belief in God. Did Washington not say, "We the people of the United States, acknowledge and admire the invisible Hand of a Divine Creator?"

Thomas Jefferson echoed this saying, "God who gave us life, gave us liberty." He then equated the belief of man in his spiritual essence with his desire for liberty. He was not wrong. The two go together. Whoever abdicates the former will easily subject himself to tyranny, because tacitly he rallies to the theory that man is no more than an object or an animal that can be directed by appropriate means toward a prescribed goal. It is a well-known tactic of all oppressors and jailers to try to break their victim's spirit.

In our days the American nation is faced with problems it has never had to face before. For two hundred years of its existence it was accustomed to an economy of abundance, made more abundant every day by its own efforts. The waves of immigrants brought with them the desire to start a new life, to escape the narrow limits of the Old World. As soon as anyone set foot on the Land of Liberty, he unconsciously was participating in this feverish search for a better life which was defined by material values. The new nation amazed the Old World by its ingenuity, its zeal, its pragmatic spirit. Technological advances never ceased in this country; they made the Americans the leading nation of the modern world. Now, all of a sudden it is jolted into the awareness that this unlimited growth might be curtailed or stopped by shortages of raw materials. Americans might be required to give up some or many of the luxuries they regarded in the past as granted, natural. It is not impossible that our standard of living will have to be reduced.

The question remains, in the face of the new situation, will America start on the way of decline, or on the contrary, will it profit from the new situation to eliminate some of the evil effects of uncontrolled material growth and become healthier, better both physically and from a moral point of view? Individuals and nations react differently to adversity; adversity may crush them or may make them stronger.

America will, I am convinced, become healthier, if it interprets the present difficulties as a welcome turn away from unbounded materialism, toward greater unity in a spiritual life. It is urgent to restore the splendor of some of the old values that were neglected in the long search for greater and greater prosperity. Those who proclaimed that "God is dead!" might now awaken to the fact that it is high time to resurrect Him in their hearts. If prosperity can no longer be attained easily, faith is within everyone's reach; it will offer us more than a mere substitute for money. A newly retrieved faith will turn material setbacks into moral blessings; when money is no longer god, then God will again lead our lives toward inner harmony, fraternity and a wonderful balance of our material, intellectual and moral aspirations.

It is probable that the present crisis of raw materials which is liable to slow down material progress will be overcome within a relatively short period. Human ingenuity will find substitutes for those items that are in short supply, but we can use the interval between a renascent prosperity and the present crisis by rediscovering the faith in the Creator, that faith that gives us dignity, a meaning to our lives, wisdom to live well and to die well, values that can not be measured, that are intangible but without which material possesions are but the polished frame to the empty canvas of our existence.

It is preposterous to say that science is incompatible

with faith. Goethe, who was a great scientist and a great poet, said, speaking about God:

> Who dare express Him?
> And who profess Him,
> Saying: I believe in Him!
> The All-enfolding,
> The All-upholding,
> Folds and upholds He not
> Thee, me, Himself?
> Arches not there the sky above us?
> And rise not, on us shining,
> Friendly, the everlasting stars?*

Einstein, like Goethe, was searching for the secret of the universe, to discover "what holds the world together in its inner structure." He came up with the field theory, the tentative answer of a giant mind to his giant question. All answers must be tentative, and this is what gives joy and thrill to the searcher. Indeed, all answers will be eventually superseded by new ones, because the great design of the universe can never be completely grasped by the human mind; consequently all search represents a climbing, a step to higher understanding. Einstein knew that he, like Goethe, was filled with awe of the All-Embracer, in whose justice and kindness he firmly believed.

Happy are those who do not lose their faith just because they discover inalterable laws of nature. The astronauts of Apollo 8 should be credited not only with being the first men to see the backside of the moon, but also for the spiritual lesson they taught us, which lesson perhaps transcends the technological achievement. For in their greatest triumph, they focused our attention on God. As they accomplished their difficult and complex mission, they were not overwhelmed by their own power; instead, at the

---

*From Goethe's FAUST. Translated by Bayard Taylor. *The Modern Library*, New York, Scene XVI, page 132.

height of their success, they displayed a humility that is so often forgotten in these days of progress. As they circled the moon they recognized that without God there would be no universe. While still in space they referred to the opening verses of the Book of Genesis, reminding us that God is the Creator of the universe, and that without His assistance, without His help, no mission, no task can be executed and fulfilled.

Again, during the Apollo 11 mission, when Edwin E. Aldrin discussed the symbolic aspects of the moon flight, he ended his remarks with a verse from the Psalms, "When I considered Thy heavens, the work of Thy fingers, the moon and the stars which Thou hast ordained, what is man that Thou art mindful of him? . . ." (Psalm 8:4-5). (Incidentally, is there not a striking resemblance between Goethe's thought and verses and the words of the Psalms? We know that the prologue of Goethe's *Faust* was inspired by the Book of Job. He was an assiduous reader of the Psalms.)

Our nation, having concluded its most significant project in space reaffirmed that we are a nation under God. Compare Aldrin's reaction to the overwhelming sight of outer space with that of the late Soviet astronaut Yuri Gagarin: "If there were a God, I would have seen him hovering somewhere in space!" Humility in the former, arrogance in the latter: which of the two men was greater? Which of the two felt greater satisfaction at the success of his endeavor? Which of the two statements represents a loftier expression of the meaning of man's striving to understand?

Faith, people will say, cannot be forced upon anyone. You either have it or you don't. This is true, but it is also true that faith in man's higher destiny, latent in all of us, can be killed by a conscious and sustained effort to inculcate unbelief into young minds. This is what is happening in Communist countries. Human beings are brought up there in the doctrine that material prosperity is the supreme goal of human life, and that this goal can and will be attained by the proper organization of society. If ever this goal is attained—they are far from it yet—it will reduce mankind to ants in an antheap, each person doing his or her job, interchangeable numbers, cogs in a machine. Woe to anyone who would dare to think that life has for him or for her no meaning; such a person would be ill-viewed and ill-treated and ultimately expelled from the human community. Dostoevski, in his poem, "The Grand Inquisitor," characterizes such a future in these terms:

> Receiving bread from us, they will see clearly that we take the bread made by their hands from them, to give it to them, without any miracle. They will be more thankful for taking it from our hands than for the bread itself. Too, too well they know the value of complete submission! . . . Oh, we shall persuade them at last not to be proud. We shall show them that they are weak, that they are only pitiful children, but that childlike happiness is the sweetest of all. . . . We shall set them to work, but in their leisure hours we shall make their life like a child's game, with children's songs and innocent dance. . . . Peacefully they will die, and beyond their grave they will find nothing but death.*

Dostoevski predicted that men will run out of such a paradise, made for them by their rulers. Yet, on the other end of the spectrum, our society is heading in the same direction as long as God, too hastily buried by our young rebels, will not be resurrected to hold vigil over our lives. Aldous Huxley, to whom I have already referred, paints a dismal picture of a society that has reached the ultimate in utilitarianism. The Brave New World of which he speaks produces human beings in the laboratory figuring out exactly how many are needed at every stage of production,

---

*Fyodor Dostoyevsky, *The Brothers Karamazov*, (Random House, The Modern Library, 1950), pp. 307, 308 (quoted in part).

from the leaders down to the scavengers. Each social class is conditioned to be satisfied, each individual is taught to believe that his is the best place in the best of the worlds. Individual thinking is only possible to the extent it contributes to the production and to the maintenance of public order; beyond that it is made impossible, for the intelligence level of everyone is determined by the proportion of the ingredients he receives in his bottle before birth. And the picture of such a humanity is exactly the same as painted by Dostoevski: it is one of total submission and of childlike happiness. However, just as predicted by the Russian author, a mistake is made and a rebel is born who thinks on his own; he incites people to run out of this earthly paradise. He is overwhelmed, life in the Brave New World continues as before . . . but the question remains, for what purpose?

Pity the societies in which the elite cannot see the presence of the Creator in the perfect harmony of the celestial bodies. The Gagarins took into outer space the emptiness they had within them. They are incapable of enjoying the almost superhuman joy that prompted the American astronauts to sing the praises of the Creator. Pity also the society which worships money as the supreme good; it is bound to be ruined by its own accomplishments. Every technological advance will require new adjustments on the part of the citizens; insecurity will increase, unhappiness will be a characteristic corollary of progress . . . unless the latter will be put in the service of ethical and religious values.

The following story is an apt commentary on the ramifications of our technical achievements. A pilot was reported to have made this announcement to his passengers, "Ladies and gentlemen, we are off course but we are making excellent time." Whether or not this story is true, it reflects the trend of our time. The speed at which we travel has led our nation to land on the moon. The tempo of our time leads us to produce a staggering volume of commodities of almost infinite variety. Thus it appears that speed and production have become national goals. However, as the above story indicates, it seems proper and fitting to ask, are we, as a nation, off course?

Long ago when the Psalmist prayed to the Lord, it was not for speed he pleaded, but to "Make the way straight before me" (Psalm 5:9). Thus, for King David, right "direction" was more important than "speed." Similarly, even in a time and especially in a time of amazing accomplishments, we must remember that, as we move ahead, we must be sure that we are moving in the right direction. Abraham Lincoln indicated that direction when he said, "I am concerned to know not whether the Lord is on my side but whether I am on the Lord's side." As long as our nation keeps this direction in mind, it will continue progress in technology and it will reconcile this progress with progress in human relations, a task of which we almost despair if we look at the present stage of the world. Nationalism in its most virulent form is rampant, the increasing perfection of weapons threatens to blow up the globe, and mankind is in danger of committing suicide. It is high time to turn away from the new idols and redirect man's attention to the Supreme Being, the only true and lasting good that never disappoints.

A last remark: it is necessary to emphasize that man is free to turn over a new leaf. It is not true that what always has been will always be, a sophistry that is often applied to the inevitability of wars among nations and groups. It is possible and urgent for every one of us to establish a sound relationship with God. To quote Dr. Victor Frankl, a great psychologist, who even in the hell of the concentration camps never abdicated his belief in the dignity of man and who survived thanks to his awareness that faith was sustaining him, "Either man's freedom of decision for or against God, as well as for or against man, must be recognized, or else religion is a delusion, and education an illusion. Freedom is presupposed by both, otherwise they are misconceived."

NO INVOLVEMENT

When I was a young boy, my father used to tell me about events that happened during the First World War.

"The war dragged on year after year, and every day life became sadder, more and more families mourned one of their beloved; hunger and cold were permanent in every household. All this was hard to bear, but we were slowly getting used to the deterioration of life. At the end of the year 1915, one day our congregation received a letter from Turkey via Rumania. It was secretly sent out of that country by a Jewish merchant of Constantinople and addressed 'to his Jewish brethren abroad.'"

My father told me so often about that letter that its contents have remained vivid in my memory. The anonymous sender described the horrors of the massacre of Armenians in Constantinople and in other cities. Night after night the Turkish police, headed by the army, descended on the Armenian quarter and systematically murdered the people there. They went from house to house, killing everyone, men, women and children, infants and old. The quarter was surrounded so that the intended victims were unable to flee.

"This massacre," the letter continued, "is still going on and will continue unless the outside world intervenes. The Armenians who live among the Turks, Jews or Greeks must hide their identities; none of them can get any bread rations nor buy any food, let alone can they find employment. We Jews," the letter added, "cannot remain indifferent to this wholesale killing of innocent people. Our religious tradition is based on the respect of human lives. In God's name we beseech our brethren to inform the world of this genocide, the horror of which defies imagination."

Similar reports were received by other congregations and were forwarded to influential newspapers in several countries. By the beginning of the year 1916 the report on the Turkish atrocities was published, and on February 17, 1916, the United States sent a formal note of protest to Turkey. I do not know whether the note remained without answer; it certainly remained without effect. Through channels that were established, our part of Europe remained in contact with Jews and Armenians in Turkey. We learned that the massacres continued, that privations and famine imposed upon the Armenians added to the death list.

"That news shook me," my father said, "more than anything that happened around us during the war. I mourned not only for the victims, but also for the killing of the spirit, for the offense made to God, that this racial massacre represented in my eyes. God had departed from among the murderers, and my heart was heavy."

I have given a great deal of thought to the story of this first genocide in Europe as related by my father. According to the various reports close to eight hundred thousand Armenians perished as a result of the persecution perpetrated by the Turks. Today, after I myself witnessed the systematic murdering and degradation of my own race, I fully understand and admire the humanity of my father, his presentiment that the Turkish example would spread to Europe, a mortal danger to Judeo-Christian religious teachings, a deadly menace to our civilization. The world then, aside from the protest by the United States, chose to ignore this monstruous crime; the world paid very dearly for its indifference. In less than a generation another global war, even more atrocious and more horrible, visited mankind. It was a new test of human solidarity and it failed.

On December 16, 1941, the *Struma*, a one-hundred-eighty ton Rumanian vessel, which normally carried a hundred passengers on coastal runs, had picked up seven hundred sixty-nine refugees from the Rumanian port of Constanza, and though none of the passengers possessed permits to disembark from the British, which had the power over Palestine, the ship began its slow voyage toward the port of Haifa. Greatly overloaded and additionally endangered by a leaking hull and defective engines, it remained at sea seventy-four days because the British did not allow the passengers to disembark, and one country after another refused to admit the unfortunate victims of Nazi persecution. Off Istanbul the ship broke down, and water poured in. The captain notified the port authorities that his ship was not seaworthy; nevertheless the Turks refused the landing permits because these were conditioned upon British certificates for Palestine which the British refused.

On February 24, 1942, the Turks towed the *Struma* to sea, well aware of the inevitable fate that awaited it. Before the vessel faded from view the people ashore read the large banner made by the passengers which said, "SAVE US!"

Six miles from the shore the *Struma* sank. Seventy children, two hundred sixty-nine women and four hundred twenty-eight men drowned. Immediately after the *Struma's* departure, local British officials received authorization from their superiors to issue Palestine certificates to the seventy children aboard.

The world was shocked, but the British government remained unmoved. Lord Cranborne, secretary of state for the colonies, taking note of the emotional reaction of some Englishmen to the tragedy, issued the following statement, a real gem in the collection of revolting utterances reflecting indifference to human suffering: "Under the present unhappy situation in the world it is to a certain extent inevitable that we should be hardened to horrors."

There was anger among good people in the rest of the world, but no official reaction to this awful tragedy was forthcoming from the responsible leaders of the free world.

Recently they built a bridge in Istanbul to connect Europe to Asia. They have not built a bridge linking human hearts to human hearts. One can imagine, as it is described in old ballads, the souls of the eight hundred thousand Armenians, of the close to eight hundred Jews, hovering over the waters of the Bosporus, lamenting their lives cut short because of the heartlessness of men. The traveler standing on that bridge, thinking of those unfortunates, must shudder with fear and sadness realizing the emptiness and senselessness of the life of humans who throw away man's most precious possession, the ability to identify one's self with others, the divine spirit in us.

I have related the story of the Hungarian Jews whose lives were offered by Eichmann to the Western Allies in exchange for war materials. Let us compare their fate with that of other Hungarian refugees, those who fled Communist tyranny after the Hungarian revolution in 1956. They were accepted everywhere, regardless of quotas and immigration laws. They were given food, medical attention, clothes, blankets, all that was necessary. They were taken to the homes of hospitable citizens; churches organized collections in their behalf; they were installed in apartments completely furnished, including television sets; they were trained for employment and the skilled workers among them were immediately offered jobs. Universities prepared special language courses for them to facilitate their adjustment to their host countries. For once, the civilized world set aside rules and regulations to listen to the voices of human decency and solidarity. One certainly approves of such reception, but one cannot help asking, "Why was the same not extended to six million Jews, precious human beings who would certainly have made a good contribution to the economy and culture of the countries that offered a refuge to them? Why were they allowed to die under the most degrading circumstances?"

As for the United States, not only did the government exercise gerat caution in dealing with Hitler, but it refused to enlarge the quota for Polish nationals in 1939 when Germany overran Poland. Keeping the status quo, insofar as the immigration law was concerned, meant that the doors of America remained locked and that appreciable numbers of either Polish Jews or Gentiles could find no refuge in this country. When the Quakers campaigned in Congress (in 1939) to bring twenty thousand children (Jewish and non-Jewish) to the United States, the Administration's inaction was largely responsible for its failure. But when, after the fall of France, England was threatened with possible invasion by the Nazis, the U. S. government quickly issued visas for ten thousand English children. When Jewish leaders negotiated with Rumania and Hungary about the emigration of their Jewish subjects with the view to bringing a considerable number of them to the United States, the American government refused to change its policy. As late as August 1, 1942, at a time when about one and a half million European Jews were already dead, the State Department insisted on verifying the reports submitted by Rabbi Stephen Wise, then president of the American Jewish Congress, to the effect that the Nazis were murdering Jews in Russia and in Poland. Checking the reports took more than three months. In the meantime more Jews perished. Finally, in November, 1942, when the reports were confirmed, the U. S. government joined the other Allied nations in a declaration entitled, "German Policy of Extermination of the Jewish Race," issued on December 17, 1942, which stated that the responsible perpetrators should not escape retribution. Although the framers of this declaration were earnest and sincere, and no doubt eager to alleviate Jewish misery, the Nazis were hardly impressed with it. This manifestation of good will came too late. By the end of 1942, many more Jews had been liquidated by the Nazis. There was a conference on refugees in Bermuda on April 19, 1942, yet neither Great Britain nor the U. S. A. was ready to admit the victims of Nazism. It was on June 12, 1944, almost five years after the launching of the extermination program, that the U. S. President, Franklin Delano Roosevelt, announced in a message to Congress "that America would bring to its shores one thousand refugees, mostly women and children, who had escaped to southern Italy." Once again Rabbi Stephen Wise worked out a secret plan (in 1944) for smuggling out Jews in exchange for bribes to be deposited in Switzerland. Seventy thousand lives could have been saved. Roosevelt gave the plan his full support and Morgenthau backed it immediately, but the State Department then held up matters for months. The British Ministry of Economic Warfare was informed and wrote back saying that "the British Foreign Office is concerned with the difficulty of disposing of any considerable number of Jews should they be released from enemy territory!"

Ultimately, according to Rabbi Stephen Wise, nothing was done owing to the shocking delay and indifference for five full months after the license had been approved by the president of the United States, the secretary of State, and the secretary of the Treasury.

The following story illustrates the attitude of the free world towards the annihilation of six million innocent victims by godless Nazi criminals.

"At a very important trial, the jury was out for deliberations to decide its verdict. After a long absence, the jurors finally returned to the courtroom. The judge asked, 'Gentlemen of the jury, have you reached your verdict?' And the foreman rose to declare, 'Yes, your Honor, we have decided *not to get involved.*'"

The last four words sounded like the death sentence of the victims; these four words gave a free hand to their executioners. This stand of no involvement raises a number of questions. Why had the two great powers, Britain and the United States, done so little to halt the process of extermination? The answers varied. Some assumed that the Western powers did not want to threaten the Germans with retaliation lest they be suspected of waging a "Jewish" war. One may then ask, what was World War II about? Was it not a fight against the dehumanizing forces, the greatest threat against civilization since the beginnings of human history? By letting the Nazis commit crimes, we did involve ourselves, but in a negative way; our fight in the cause of human freedom lost much of its authenticity by the fact of abandoning millions of human beings to the cruelty of beasts with human faces. Others maintained that from the vantage point of diplomacy a defense of the Jews would have hindered the plans of invasion. But no sound answer was given to the question about the stubborn British refusal to open the gates of Palestine to Jewish escapees and about the Mandatory government's practice of imprisoning in detention camps in Cyprus and in Palestine those who reached the shores of the Jewish National Home without bonafide certificates of immigration. Yet, as Abba Eban, the former foreign minister of Israel points out in his book, *The Story of My People*, by 1943 Palestine was safe from invasion.* Abba Eban further states that it was believed that the most urgent task was then to create a favorable climate for a post-war settlement in Palestine. At this point one cannot help asking, why did the Jewish leaders of the time concern themselves with post-war problems when thousands and thousands of Jews were murdered daily? Why did they not rather dedicate all their efforts toward the goal of rescuing Jewish lives?

Next to the question concerning the attitude of the Allied governments towards the victims of Nazism, arises an even more painful question: why organized religion kept silent in the face of what was happening in countries under the boots of the Nazis? To be sure, some church officials, acting in the spirit of Christian charity, opened their cloisters and monasteries to harried Jews, but these righteous acts were isolated instances, exceptions to the rule. The fact is that no official representation was ever made by the heads of Christian churches, nor by the spokesmen of Islam and Buddhism which could have expressed in the strongest

---

*Abba Eban, *The Story of My People* (New York: Random House, 1968), p. 424.

possible terms the protest of all true believers. While the death factories operated at full blast, the papacy itself was silent. The silence of the Pope has been the subject of debate ever since the end of World War II. The playwright Rolf Hochhuth expressed the view in his play, *The Deputy*, that the Pope's failure to speak out against Nazi brutalities should be considered as telling evidence of his indifference to the plight of the Jews and thus a serious moral lapse. In "Sidelines on History," the appendix to his play, Hochhuth writes, "It remains incomprehensible that His Holiness did not bestir himself to protest against Hitler, when it was clear that Germany had lost the war, while at the same time Auschwitz was just beginning its highest daily quota of killings."

Other writers are not as ready to blacken the character of the Pope. Leon Poliakov, one of the outstanding researchers of the holocaust, finds an explanation for the silence of Pius XII. He writes, "The immense church interests which were the Pope's responsibility, the extensive means for blackmail which the Nazis enjoyed on a scale commensurate with the Universal Church, probably account for his failure to issue that solemn and public declaration which the persecuted looked forward to so ardently."

As for the intellectual community of the free world, save for a number of sporadic denunciations by some writers, scientists and academicians, the majority did not raise their voices in protest against Nazi genocide. The academic communities did not react en masse in a collective *j'accuse*. The pen clubs of the world did not sow the seed of revolt in the 1930s when outside of Germany it was still possible to arouse the people against Nazi theory and practice. They did not issue proclamations calling upon millions of readers to stand up and be heard. There were few anti-Nazi rallies conducted by the intellectuals on the campuses, in public forums and there was little utilization of the mass media for the purpose of informing the public of the Hitlerite menace.

Reactions of the liberals and progressives in the labor movement and in socio-cultural organizations were in sympathy and solidarity with the suffering Jews, but these feelings were not translated in terms of positive actions on their behalf. Had the multitudes in the free world reacted courageously and vigorously, many of the Nazi acts of terror might have been averted.

The Jewish communities themselves, in countries not overrun by the Nazis, lacked any mass reaction to the horrible news concerning their coreligionists across the ocean. It has been pointed out by students of the holocaust period that most Jewish people could not believe the reports which reached them from the ghettos of Europe. To be sure, these reports sounded incredible, passing human understanding; but when they were confirmed, they had a paralyzing effect upon most of them. Furthermore, the loyalty of Jews as citizens of free countries made them sensitive to the plea not to hamper the war effort by any "exaggerated" demands. Thus, rescue activities were confined to the philanthropic agencies and to the Palestinian Jews through the Jewish Agency. In America, the anti-Nazi boycott conducted by the Joint Boycott Council, which resulted in a decline of Germany's place in the world economy,* and the anti-Nazi campaign carried out by various organizations were efforts to unmask the true face of the Nazis and to combat mounting anti-Jewish feelings on the American continent. But the masses of Jews in the U. S. and in other free lands did not make extrordinary efforts to impress on their governments that official reaction doomed their brethren to certain death. During the period of 1933 to 1945—during the Hitler era—there were no sit-ins nor mass demonstrations in the dense population centers. There were no marches of Jewish masses to Washington, Ottawa, London, Johannesburg, Buenos Aires, and Rio de Janeiro. The majority of the Jewish people during the period of the

---

*See *The New York Times,* March 28, 1934.

great catastrophe did not tremble sufficiently to inject a chill into the hearts of their Christian neighbors.

Thus, one can see, every organization, every segment of the society of the free world was equally guilty of washing their hands of the fate of six million lives. The survivors of those times may have washed their hands throughout their lives, but they will never become clean again. Yet, and this must be emphasized, *the greatest responsibility* for this unprecendented mass murder of history *lies with Stalin and other leaders of the Soviet Union.* Stalin was adamant in forbidding any negotiations with the Germans with a view of saving hundreds of thousands, perhaps millions of Jewish lives from the clutches of the Nazis. Stalin, who prior to the German attack on Russia had been an ally of Germany, was liable to switch again and rejoin the camp of the enemies of the Allies, which could have spelled the ruin of the Western world. Churchill was mortally afraid of this and because of this, he made sacrifices that he was loathe to make. Because of Stalin's veto, Great Britain foiled the negotiations and induced the United States to cancel military operations against the concentration camps.

The history of World War II furnishes other examples that illustrate Stalin's complete indifference to the sacrifice of human lives.

In 1943 the Polish government-in-exile in London and the Soviet regime came to an open breach as a consequence of the discovery by Polish peasants of mass graves of Polish officers in the forest of Katyn, near Smolensk. Stalin then rejected any knowledge of this massacre and accused the Germans of having been the authors of the same. The Poles knew who was responsible for these murders; Western historians were not sure, but now the guilt of Stalin is established,* though the reason remains obscure.

---

*The Columbia History of the World, edited by John A. Garraty and Peter Gay. Harper & Row, publishers (New York, Evanston, San Francisco, London), 1972.

This crime is, by the way, in keeping with Stalin's attitude toward the abortive Warsaw uprising of August, 1944. The Red Army was then at the gates of the Polish capital. The Polish government-in-exile had, through its emissaries, organized it down to the smallest detail, notifying the commanders of the Red Army of the forces that were to attack the Germans in the city. The liberation of Warsaw was to begin the cleansing of Polish territory of the German occupant, and the beginning of the liberation of all other countries occupied by them. Stalin, however, did not want the exiled Polish government to be credited with the liberation of their capital. He had other plans. He refused to assist, or permit to be assisted, the people of Warsaw fighting the Nazis. The Red Army stood by, allowing the troops of Hitler to crush the Poles. By the first days of October, the freedom fighters were annihilated. The Hitlerite soldiery avenged themselves on the population. Most of the inhabitants of the city were massacred, and the city was looted and almost completely destroyed. During all those days Stalin's army was standing by, separated only by the river from the enraged Nazis. The order it received was: *no involvement.* Let hundreds of thousands of people perish by the bullets of the Nazis. Let women and children be beaten to death, houses set afire, monuments, museums, works of art, schools and buildings that represented the efforts of generations crumble. This was political planning. The fact that Stalin thought of establishing a Communist government in Poland, prevailed over purely humanitarian considerations or loyalty to the Allies. This affair created consternation in the West; it exceeded anything that the Western powers believed to be possible, and laid bare the unreliability of Stalin as an ally. It produced a real, though not publicized crisis in the Big Three Alliance. Fortunately, the German military might was in its last throes; the end of the war was near.

Stalin's grim record of inhumanity is further blackened by his treatment of the Soviet prisoners of war who returned home after the defeat of Germany. They were treated like traitors. The Soviet authorities would not examine the reasons why an individual soldier or a group of soldiers had surrendered to the Germans; they would not bother with individual cases. Many war heroes, defenders of Sevastopol, Odessa, and Brest, partisans, people who had been tortured in Nazi camps, were sent to Soviet concentration camps. The writer Solzhenitsyn eloquently describes in his books, *One Day in the Life of Ivan Denisovich, The First Circle,* and *The Cancer Ward,* the atmosphere and the population of those camps. Stalin was even indifferent to the fate of his own son, Jacob. The latter was taken prisoner at the beginning of the war. After Stalingrad, the Germans proposed to exchange him for Field Marshall Friedrich Paulus, commander of the Army that was captured by the Russians at Stalingrad. Stalin refused and Jacob was shot by the Nazis.

Political expediency prompted the Western Allies not to get involved in the saving of six million Jews, but with Stalin there was still another consideration: his inveterate anti-semitism. The latter might go back to his rivalry with Trotsky, the Jewish companion of struggle of Lenin, whose two names were associated in the beginning of the Communist revolution. At a time when Stalin's own name was still comparatively unknown, it is history that Trotsky was exiled by Stalin and assassinated on Stalin's order in Mexico. My own experience, as I told it in previous chapters of this book, taught me that the deportees who had escaped from the Nazi camps could not count on any assistance on the part of the Red Army. On the contrary, if I had not escaped from the Russians after having slipped away from my column of forced laborers, I might have perished somewhere in a camp in Siberia, without anyone knowing where I vanished and what my crime was to deserve such a fate.

One event, commemorated by the Russian poet Yevtushenko and described by another writer, A. Anatoli (Kuznetsov), the story of Babi Yar, links as no other gruesome episode of World War II, the Nazis and the Communists through their utter disregard and contempt of the value of human lives.

Kuznetsov, then a boy of thirteen, lived in that year of 1941 in Kiev, in the Ukraine, which the German Army occupied after a long struggle. During the German advance in Russia, the Jews were not alarmed as to their fate at the hand of the occupants. Indeed, as Kuznetsov relates,* right up to the German attack on the Soviet Union, Russian newspapers had been praising and glorifying Hitler as the Soviet Union's best friend, and had been silent about German atrocities against the Jews. It was therefore for them a thunderclap from a blue sky when they read stuck on fences after the entry of the Germans into Kiev, the following notice:

> "All Yids living in the city of Kiev and its vicinity are to report by 8 o'clock on the morning of Monday, September 29, 1941, at the corner of Melnikovsky and Dokhturov Streets [near the cemetery]. They are to take with them documents, money, valuables, as well as warm clothes, underwear, etc. Any Yid not carrying out this instruction and who is found elsewhere will be shot."

> They started arriving while it was still dark, to be in good time to get seats in the train. With their howling children, their old and sick, some of them weeping, the Jews who lived and worked on the vegetable farm emerged onto the street. There were bundles roughly tied together with string, worn-out cases made from plywood, woven baskets, boxes of carpenters' tools. Some elderly women were wearing strings of onions hung around their necks like gigantic necklaces—food supplies for the journey.

> I was struck by how many sick and unfortunate people there are in the world. . . .

---

*A. Anatoli (Kuznetsov), *Babi Yar* (New York: Farrar, Straus and Giroux, 1970), pp. 94ff., 470ff.

When I got home I found my grandfather standing in the middle of the courtyard, straining to hear some shooting that was going on somewhere. He raised his finger.
"Do you know what?" he said with horror in his voice. "They are not deporting 'em. They're shooting 'em."

Some seventy-five thousand Jews were shot in the first few weeks in Kiev and its surroundings. Babi Yar—the ravine called Babi—received the bones of most of them. The Communists were, of course, innocent of this monstruous crime, but after the war they made extraordinary efforts in order to efface the memory of Babi Yar from the conscience of the world. Indeed, these efforts were so great that they could not have been any greater had the Communists committed the crime themselves. Here is what Kuznetsov tells about this:

> As soon as the war ended, people—of whom Ilya Ehrenburg was one of the first—started saying that a memorial should be erected at Babi Yar. But the Central Committee of the Ukrainian Communist Party, of which Nikita Krushchev was then in charge, considered that the people who had been executed in Babi Yar did not deserve the memorial.
> More than once I heard Communists in Kiev saying this sort of thing, "What Babi Yar are you talking about? Where they shot the Yids? And who said we had to put a memorial up to some lousy Yids?"
> In fact, with the spread of government-inspired anti-Semitism between 1948 and 1953, the question of erecting a monument was dropped.
> After Stalin's death people again started cautiously putting round the view that Babi Yar was in fact not just a Jewish grave and that there were three or four times as many people in it of Russian and other nationalities. But the Ukrainian Central Committee, headed in 1957 by Nikolai Podgorny, apparently worked

out the percentages, found them unconvincing and arrived at a Solomon-like solution—to put a stop once and for all to talk about Babi Yar, to destroy it and forget all about it.

That marked the beginning of the second attempt to erase Babi Yar from history.

To fill in such an enormous ravine was a gigantic task, but it was possible, given the vast scale of construction work in the U.S.S.R. The engineers hit on a very clever solution—to fill the ravine not by tipping but washing earth into it by means of pumping machinery. They built a dam across the end of Babi Yar and proceeded to pump pulp—a mixture of water and mud—into it through pipes from the neighboring quarries of brickworks. The ravine was turned into a lake. The idea was that the mud would separate and settle, while the water would flow away through channels in the dam. The water in the lake was evil-smelling, green and stagnant, and the noise of the pulp pouring out of the pipes went on day and night. That lasted for several years. Each year the dam was strenghtened and increased in height, until by 1961 it was the height of a six-story building.

On Monday, March 13, 1961, it collapsed. The spring rains had rushed down into the ravine and filled the lake to overflowing; the channels could not deal with the volume of water and it went right over the top of the dam.

At first the water flooded the roadway, so that trams and cars were halted. People were hurrying to work at the time, and crowds gathered on both sides of the road, unable to get across.

At 8:45 in the morning there was a frightful roar, and a wall of liquid mud thirty feet high poured out of the mouth of Babi Yar. Eye-witnesses who managed to escape and who watched from a distance affirm that the wall of mud burst out of the ravine with the speed of an express train, that no one could get out of its way and that the cries of hundreds of people were smothered in half a minute.

Whole crowds of people were swallowed up instantly in the wave of mud. People sitting in trams and in their cars perished, presumably without having time to grasp what had happened. There was no question of anybody being able to work his way to the surface of that glutinous mass, or of getting free, however much he floundered about in it.

Houses which stood in the way of the wave were swept away as if made of cardboard. A few trams were carried along by it a couple of hundred yards and then buried. So were the tram terminus, the hospital, the stadium, an instrument factory and the whole of the residential quarter. . . .

The sea of mud which had spread far and wide had at last an opportunity of drying out and hardening as the water gradually seeped out of it in little rivulets down to the Dnieper, and in the late spring it became possible to start clearing it.

The digging went on for two years and resembled the excavation of Pompeii. A great many bodies were recovered—in the houses, in their beds, in air pockets formed beneath the ceilings in rooms. One person had been making a call in a telephone booth, and perished there, with the receiver in his hand. At the tram terminus they dug out a group of conductors who had just gathered to hand over their takings, along with the cashier who was taking the money over. The number of people who perished was, of course, never stated. Babi Yar was never lucky with figures.

The phrase "Babi Yar takes its revenge" was then much on people's lips. The main feature of the Bolshevik character however, is a reluctance ever to give up.

The third, and most serious attempt started in 1962. A tremendous quantity of machinery was brought into

Babi Yar—excavators, bulldozers, tipping lorries and earth-moving machines. The soil was moved back into the ravine, some of it was spread over the area that had been destroyed, and Babi Yar was finally filled in and a main road carried across it. Then the following works were undertaken:

On the place where the concentration camp had been they built a whole new complex of multi-story dwelling-houses, built them on bones, as you might say. When they were digging the foundations, they kept coming across bones, sometimes caught in the barbed wire. The windows and balconies of the first rows of these houses look out over the very place where the mass executions of the Jews took place in 1941.

Reading this description of the extraordinary efforts of the Soviet authorities to erase the memory of Babi Yar, it is impossible not to ask, why did they divert the talents and the materials of construction from other projects, at a time when a very large part of the Soviet Union lay in ruins and had to be rebuilt? Obviously, there was a powerful psychological reason behind that decision. The gigantic works undertaken at Babi Yar, the sacrifices consented to erase a crime of history can be explained only by the fact that the Soviet leaders themselves felt guilty of similar crimes. Their intervention at Babi Yar aimed at not letting the outside world involve themselves with this and other mass murders committed on their orders. It was an effort to promote *no involvement*. However, the twenty-odd million peasants from whom the grain was taken on Stalin's orders, and who starved to death as a result of this,[*] the Polish freedom fighters who were allowed to die because of Stalin's politics, the six million Jews for whose death the Soviet Union was indirectly responsible, all confirm this judgment of the author of Babi Yar:

---
[*]Roy A. Medvedev, *Let History Judge* (New York: Alfred A. Knopf, 1972), pp. 62, 66.

"However much you burn and disperse and cover over and trample down, human memory still remains. History cannot be deceived, and it is impossible to conceal anything from it for ever."

A last word about involvement or the opposite of it. Every state that was moved by humanitarian consideration and opened its doors to the victims of persecution, has always benefited from it. It is practical policy to be humane; the refugees generally work hard and enhance the economy, enrich the culture of the host country. By contrast, an attitude of indifference toward the fates of victims of persecution inevitably engenders the breakdown of international morality and endangers the peace of the world. The events that occurred since the end of World War II amply demonstrate this fact. When it is generally understood and when all the civilized world derives the conclusions from this truth, the day will come when the nations establish a code of international obligations toward the oppressed, the persecuted. A new era of fraternal concern, of the realization of what Martin Buber, the great Jewish existentialist called, "I Am Thou!" will then herald the emergence of a better world. For it has been abundantly proven and recognized by those who have eyes to see and ears to hear, hearts to feel and minds to think, that only love, the love of our fellowmen, well-conceived self-love, and—in religious terms —the love of God can maintain human society together. The weapons manufactured by human ingenuity become ever more sophisticated, and the more sophisticated they become, the more the world becomes insecure. We must all be involved not in the business of forging weapons against each other, but in that of making weapons unnecessary.

In conclusion, it is worth repeating the words of George W. Cecil appearing in an advertisement in *American Magazine*, who said, "On the Plains of Hesitation bleach the bones of countless millions who, at the Dawn of Victory, sat down to wait—and waiting, died."

BELOW THE SURFACE—BEYOND THE HORIZON: DÉTENTE OR SUBTERFUGE?

The principle of no involvement was made the basis of international politics in 1945 by the Yalta and Potsdam agreements. These two international treaties divided the world into spheres of interest, the Western powers to exercise their influence on Western Europe and Japan, while the Soviet Union to become supreme in Eastern Europe, the Balkans, Poland and what we now call Eastern Germany. Indeed, defeated Germany was divided then into four occupation zones—U.S., British, French and Soviet. The three Western powers construed the Potsdam agreement to the effect that eventually the four zones would be reunited into a peace-loving, democratic state, following free elections.

The interpretation of the Soviet Union was a different one. Everywhere in its sphere of interest, police states were created, politics was brought under control of Communist-dominated coalitions and later under the Communist party, while a program of Sovietization was carried out. The Western powers were not supposed to interfere in accordance with the principle of no involvement. The peoples of Poland, the Soviet Occupation Zone of Germany, Bulgaria, Czechoslovakia, Hungary and Rumania, were entrapped within the walls of Communism.

No involvement is mandatory only for the Western world; within the Communist-dominated sphere, involvement is very much the rule. When the workers of Berlin or the Hungarians revolted against the barbaric treatment of the authorities, or against anyone who even by far could be suspected of not being sympathetic to Communism, when the Czechoslovak nation wished to give a more human face to the regime, the Soviet leaders involved themselves with tanks, machine guns and by every means at their disposal to put down these attempts at freedom.

Historian Arnold Toynbee, in an article published in *The Los Angeles Times* (June 24, 1973), stated that religion was "society's rockbottom basis." During my stay in Rumania after the war and ever since, I had ample opportunity to convince myself that religion was discouraged in Soviet dominated territories. I, as a rabbi, of course share Toynbee's judgment on the importance of religion for the survival of a free society; but even those who are not religious or who are agnostic, can persuade themselves of the deceit admitted as a means of international policy by the Communist rulers everywhere. Examples of such deceitful intentions abound. In Cuba, Krushchev was sending missiles capable of destroying American cities, while his ambassador went out of his way to assure President Kennedy of his country's peaceful intentions toward the United States.

Let us go back to what happened during the Hungarian uprising. When the Hungarians, under Premier Nagy, tried to free themselves from Russian occupation and forced the Russian army out of Hungary, the Hungarian chief of staff and his associates were called by the Russian army leaders on the pretext of negotiating a "peaceful settlement." The "peaceful negotiations" turned into imprisonment; the chief of staff and his associates were jailed and the Russian march into Budapest began. There was no leadership left to oppose organized resistance against the Russians.

To illustrate the sedation method copied from the Nazis by the Russians (or vice versa), I cite another example. Not too long ago Czechoslovakia was occupied by the Russians, and it came under their complete domination. Prior to the entry of Communist troops into that unhappy country, Russia made overtures of friendship to Premier Dubchek, head of the new movement of "socialism with a human face." The Russians agreed to send their representatives to meet with Dubchek on Czechoslovak territory at a small border town, named Cierna. The purpose of this visit was to convince the Czech people that the Russians had nothing but peaceful intentions toward them. To emphasize these intentions they asked for a second meeting to be held in the Slovak city of Bratislava. All these friendly gestures were aimed at lulling the Czechoslovak people into a sense of security; then, one day, the Russians mobilized the troops of their satellite countries, to give the occupation a semblance of common ideological action, and the small nation was invaded without encountering any resistance.

Now that Brezhnev is diligently working at dismantling the cold war and bringing about new relationships with the United States, I cannot help thinking of the ways by which they have circumvented all previous agreements to consolidate Communism worldwide. Not being a politician but a religious man, it is as such that I fear for this nation under God, bent upon trusting the given word even of a former adversary. Brezhnev served his apprenticeship in the same slaughterhouse as did Lenin, Stalin, Krushchev and Kosygin, and wields the same cleaver of tyranny handed down by his predecessors. Americans and Soviets interpreted the agreements concluded after the war in very different ways; for the former, they were to prepare for a free world, for the freedom of individuals and nations, while for the Communists they meant freedom from the interference by the Western powers, freedom to achieve their goals. These goals, there can be no doubt about it, are the abolition of the free choice of peoples to elect their leaders, the establishment of an anthill type of society worldwide. The present détente is, in my opinion, based on my life experience, but a subterfuge to get from the American people the technical help they urgently need; when the time is ripe, when Russia has received sufficient technological and economic assistance from us, when the Soviets no longer fear any danger to the Soviet Union, thanks to their overwhelming military superiority, then they will show their true face again. I shudder to think what that face will be.

Ancient history offers some analogies to the present world situation. The Talmud recorded a dialogue between two great scholars who lived at the height of Greek influence in the Mediterranean and on the seacoast of Africa. Rabbis Eliezer and Joshua, two famous Jewish scholars of the time, once traveled together across the sea. Rabbi Eliezer found nothing interesting to see during their journey and he closed his eyes ever so often; Rabbi Joshua however, remained alert, reacting to every minute occurrence.

Suddenly Rabbi Joshua uttered a cry. Startled, Rabbi Eliezer asked him, "What is it that you see?" Rabbi Joshua said, "I see a large light above the waters." Rabbi Eliezer smiled and said, "Look at it a little closer. You will discover that the light you see is nothing but the glimmer of the enormous, avid eyes of the Leviathan that is eager to swallow everything smaller in size than itself."

The story is an allegory of the dispute that separated the two scholars in regard to their view of the situation of the world of their time.

Rabbi Eliezer was acquainted with the leaders of the important Greek states; he realized that under the guise of spreading Greek culture, they were bent upon conquering the smaller Greek colonies. He reflected bitterly and sarcastically upon the fact that even eminent men such as Rabbi Joshua could be so easily misled. The latter had seen the light on the surface but not what hid underneath. That light, the Hellenistic movement of the time, was indeed, admirable; but the ferocious appetite for conquest which it concealed caused bloody wars among the Greeks and was responsible for their ultimate defeat by the Romans.

That parable applies to the world situation today. Many exclaim enthusiastically, "What a wonderful light of international understanding rises on the horizon!" But *Pravda*, the official organ of the Russian Communist Party, comments, "Coexistence does not mean a discontinuation of the class struggle, only the renunciation of military methods."

Krushchev's boast, "We shall bury you!" still animates the leaders of the Soviet Union. The latter is basically hostile to the United States. It would like to see a weakening of American power and influence all over the world. The light on the horizon, optimistically called "détente," the meetings between American and Russian leaders, Brezhnev's visit to the United States, did not prevent Russia from pursuing a dangerous policy in the Middle East, one which once more brought the world to the brink of World War III. She poured, and is still pouring billions of dollars worth of armaments into the Arab states, not because of any love for the cause of the Arabs, but in order to realize her long-time aim, to acquire bases in the Mediterranean and to set foot in the Indian Ocean. Had the Arabs defeated Israel, had they suceeded in erasing the Jewish state, the Russians would be in a position to lay their hands on the world's oil resources and to dictate to Europe. They would have at the same time, secured their flanks and occupied an impregnable position in Asia. The stakes were high; the expected results justified the heavy expenses. While they thus armed the Arabs, they were speaking of détente and of peaceful coexistence. At a time when Brezhnev was posing for the photographers together with American leaders, the most sophisticated Russian arms were being delivered to Egypt and Syria, in order to enable the Russians to fight by proxy, by the pawns and puppets they were moving, for their ambitious interests.

The Soviet Union tried to deal a big blow to the United States by building up the Arabs and encouraging them to use their oil as a weapon. This too, happened while it preached détente and peaceful coexistence; one must wonder what would be its attitude toward us if the hawks in the Kremlin regained the upper hand they once had among the true rulers of the Soviet Union. At any rate, one cannot trust their reassurance of good intentions for there are signs that radical changes are being prepared in Soviet military and political leadership. The veteran chief of staff, Marshall V. Zakharov, formerly a figure of immense power and authority, was first retired and then died. His successor, General V. Kulikov, is a very able professional soldier. He is relatively young, in his early fifties, and he has surrounded himself by new military leaders as young or younger than himself.

The changing of the guard has been brought about by pressure exerted on the leadership by the hawks in the Kremlin. Just as Krushchev was unexpectedly removed soon after he had to give in to the ultimatum of President Kennedy during the Cuban crisis, so could Brezhnev and his supporters be removed overnight, and a new period of cold war could begin. The recent shaking up of Soviet military leadership does not augur well for the peaceful coexistence promised by the Soviet Union.

It was not a Westerner but Andrei Sakharov, a celebrated Soviet scientist, three times cited as Hero of Socialist Labor, a member of the prestigious Soviet Academy of Sciences, who issued the loudest warning to the West not to give technological assistance to the Soviet Union without forcing a change of the police system now prevailing in that country. At a press conference that has become of historical importance in the chronicles of the fight for human rights, Sakharov made the following statement:

> I emphasize the need for mutual trust, which to be achieved, requires wide public disclosure and open-

ness in a society as well as democratization, the freedom of dissemination of information, of the exchange of ideas and respect for all basic rights of the person, particularly respect for the right to choose the country where one wishes to live.

Sakharov added that the development of the industrial potential of a police state would not further the creation of a better world and the cause of international peace; on the contrary, it would threaten these aims. "It is strange," he said, "how long it takes people to realize that one values moral principles above material things. For a long time, the [Soviet] authorities evidently thought I was up in arms simply because of career dissatisfaction or living conditions."

Sakharov does not consider himself unpatriotic. On the contrary, he is imbued with a deep love of his country. For twenty years he worked on nuclear weapons because he believed that by making the Soviet Union stronger he would promote world peace. The warning uttered by him, quoted above, shows that his opinion has changed in this regard. He is now convinced that, as the Soviet Union acquires more powerful weapons, it will use them to foster not freedom but tyranny at home as well as abroad. Indeed the cause of freedom is indivisible: a regime based on the suppression of the human rights of its own citizens cannot be but a menace to the freedom of all peoples everywhere.

Andrei Sakharov is the foremost physicist of Russia; nevertheless, he has been vilified by public attacks on his person, harassed by the Secret Police. He has lost his position of President of the Academy of Sciences and was reduced to the rank of a simple research scientist which carries a salary assuring him bare survival. Sakharov has been invited to teach for a year at Princeton University; this prospect excites his imagination yet he does not dare to accept the offer. He is convinced that if he asked for, and were given permission to go to the United States, he would never get back to Moscow. He was told by the police that he would get his passport, but that his wife would have to remain. Sakharov refused. Sakharov's conviction regarding the fate he might expect once he has left his country is confirmed by what has happened to his friend and fellow-fighter, Alexander Solzhenitsyn. The latter's story and personality have become a legend in the Western world. He was a victim of Stalin, sent to concentration camps for many years, for having written in terms less than deferential of the Tyrant. Solzhenitsyn had cancer and was cured of it. He had come back from the deepest depth of misery; he cannot be intimidated anymore. His first novel, *One Day in the Life of Ivan Denisovitch* was published in Russia, in the euphoria created by the anti-Stalinist atmosphere that followed Krushchev's speech at the Twentieth Congress of the Communist Party; but his subsequent works, *The First Circle* and *Cancer Ward,* were no longer allowed to see the light of the day in his country. Indeed the new rulers of Russia realized that the situation he castigated in his writings continued to be prevalent under them, as it had been under Stalin. They feared and hated Solzhenitsyn, yet did not dare to imprison him or confine him in an insane asylum as they had done with other dissidents, for the Western world was alerted and they could not afford to flaunt world opinion at a time when they needed an era of a so-called détente to pursue their intricate and obscure schemes in their foreign policy. The last straw that put an end to their inaction concerning Solzhenitsyn was the latter's publication abroad of his latest book, *The Gulag Archipelago,* a documentary of Soviet crimes since the establishment of the Communist Empire in Europe. This documentary encompasses the mass murders committed by the Communists in Russia as well as their wanton killings and deprivation of the liberties of millions of human beings at home and abroad. *The Gulag Archipelago* confirms and supplements Sakharov's warnings on the connection between an increase of Soviet power and the menace of greater tyranny everywhere.

After the publication of this last of his books, Solzhenitsyn, as well known, was thrown out of his country and was deprived of his citizenship. This latest arbitrary act of the Soviet government actually pays homage to Solzhenitsyn, because it proves that the Soviet leaders know how unhappy Solzhenitsyn will be in exile, no matter how great his fame. Moreover, the leaders of the Soviet Union might have believed that by exiling him, Solzhenitsyn's voice will not reach the masses in his country, a foolish belief, I am convinced of it.

Americans might heed the words of these two courageous Russians. They know more than anyone else what it means to live in an unfree country. Sakharov and Solzhenitsyn constitute the latest spearhead of dissidents, victims of the society, intolerant of intellectual dissent, fearful of new ideas, suspicious of all that fails to conform with rigid, Communist Party dogma enforced by the power and the mentality of the secret police. The list of these dissidents is already long, though not well-known outside, and even inside the Soviet Union. Where is Andrei Amalrik, the brilliant young historian, author of *Will the Soviet Union Survive Until 1984,* a book translated into English, and widely circulated in the United States thanks to its diffusion by the Book-of-the-Month Club? Where are Grigorenko, Bukovsky, Ysenin-Volpin, and many others? Sakharov gave Western correspondents the names of several dissidents and of a half a dozen hospitals, which, he said, were used to punish people on criminal trial. He charged that doctors use a depressent drug, Halopyridol, to affect their minds.

"They can make insane people out of normal people," added Mrs. Sakharov, herself a physician, also present at the news conference.

"Let the presence of the Red Cross lead to the removal of the inhuman bars over the windows of Soviet prisons and stay the criminal hands that are injecting Halopyridol into Leonid Plyushch [a friend] in the hell of Dnepropetrovsk prison mental hospital," Sakharov said.

The scientist further charged that the mental diagnoses of many dissidents as insane are false and urged Western psychiatrists, who had gathered in Moscow for a convention, to investigate specific cases. If the Soviet government claims the dissidents are sick, they should be moved to Western hospitals for treatment, Sakharov declared.

One Western correspondent succeeded in obtaining a recording of the voices of Daniel and Sinyavski, sentenced to hard labor in an isolated camp somewhere in Siberia. The voices said that the two writers were ill and not receiving medical attention; in fact, they were dying.

Two of the dissidents, Pyotr Yakir, age fifty, a historian, and Viktor Krasin, forty-four, an economist, recently appeared on the brightly lighted stage of Moscow's Journalists' Club to meet with Western newsmen. These two men had previously turned state's evidence at their secret trial, and were sentenced to three years in prison, to be followed by three years of enforced residence in a remote part of the country. (Such internal exile after the purging of his sentence by a condemned man is a Russian tradition continued since Czarist times.)

At that press conference, arranged by Soviet officials, Yakir, who once said that if he ever confessed to the secret police "it would not be the real me speaking," declared, in the presence of the first deputy prosecutor of the state, that "our activities were illegal because we knew we were breaking the law." Krasin said of their former struggle for civil rights, "We simply changed our minds."

That press conference was obviously held to warn Soviet citizens against unauthorized contacts with Western newsmen and to warn other prominent dissidents of their ultimate fate if they persisted in criticizing Soviet repression.

The trial and "confessions" of Yakir and Krasin signal a momentary triumph for the Kremlin's forces of conservative orthodoxy. However, Solzhenitsyn remained undaunted. He added an ugly postscript the next day to the public abasement of the two men. He revealed that an unpublished book he had written on Soviet labor camps had been recently seized by the secret police, who forced a woman to disclose its location through five days of uninterrupted interrogation. She subsequently hanged herself. In spite of the efforts of the secret police to suppress the book, it reached the West.

"Never in the history of any land," the author contends, "has any people suffered so much at the hands of the government as under the Soviet system."

As stated the "Gulag Archipelago" symbolizes the network of political prison camps scattered like islands across the Soviet Union. The book details the horrors of the prisons, including torture by the secret police, now known as the Committee for State Security, or KGB. The volume covers the first forty years of Soviet rule, from 1918 to 1958.

It points out that Lenin, worshipped in the Soviet Union like a saint, actually was a tyrant advocating unprecedented terror against political adversaries. The author accuses Stalin of planning a mass program against Jews in Moscow, to be followed by their mass exile to Siberia, except for those to be hanged in Red Square, a form of execution unknown since Czarist times.

Solzhenitsyn in fact estimates that Soviet repression was ten to a thousand times greater than Czarist repression, depending on whether one is talking about arrest, exile or execution. His figures for specifics are much higher than those previously cited in the West, like a suggestion that six hundred thousand people were arrested after the assassination of Sergei Kirov in 1934. He suggests also that the Russians had more victims than the Nazis.

Rousseau's *Social Contract* begins with these words: "Man was born free, yet so many men are in chains."

We could modify this, speaking of the Soviet Union: "They preached liberation and they have enslaved their people."

In fifty-five years of Soviet rule they have not learned

that man's impulse to be free will not forever be stifled. The voice of Andrei Sakharov, founder of the unofficial Committee on Human Rights, is heard not only in the West but through the hard grapevine that keeps things going in all closed societies. Virtually every intellectual and most university students have read the works of Solzhenitsyn that have been banned from publication in his own land. They have also read all or part of the historic protest manifesto published abroad by Sakharov, who has openly expressed his growing disillusionment with a system that denies scientific as well as other cultural and intellectual freedoms.

And if he is not jailed or sent into exile, Sakharov will once again head the small group of dissidents who silently protest the repression of the Kremlin by gathering each December on a small, pleasant square near the heart of Moscow, named for the great poet Pushkin, whose larger-than-life statue looks out on one of the city's principal avenues, named after the great writer Gorky. It is a symbolic convergence of history's dissidents against tyranny.

Sakharov's warning that technological advance is harmful unless it goes hand in hand with democratization and the right to choose the country where one wishes to live, has been dramatically justified with the emergence of the question of the emigration of Soviet Jews to Israel. The facts are known. The Jews who applied for a passport with a view of emigrating were to pay an exit tax, the amount of which varied according to the degree of education they had and the job they held. In every case it was calculated so high that the future emigrant was to leave almost completely destitute. Whether the passport was granted to him or not, he was from the moment of his application, thrown out of his employment, often out of his lodging, ostracized by neighbors and friends, branded a traitor to the Soviet Union. The U. S. Senate was alerted, and several of the senators, among them Senator Jackson, declared that the United States should not grant Russia the position of "most favored nation" in the trade negotiations that had been initiated between the two countries, unless she revoked the decree about the exit tax. This time the indifference and apathy, expressed by the words "No Involvement" yielded to a feeling of solidarity with people deprived of their personal freedom. The American Senate rallied around the view expressed by Senator Jackson; the position coveted by the Soviets was temporarily abandoned. Thereupon it was announced that the Soviet authorities have taken off the exit tax on emigrants; yet when the American presidential election was over in November, 1972, they put the tax back on. Then they have removed it again, or so they say. Actually no one is certain what the attitude of the Soviet authorities in regard to the exit tax is; one only knows that, while they allow a certain number of people to leave, the favor of granting a passport seems to be done arbitrarily without any specific pattern or in keeping with any regulation. Actually, the tax is just a cover for a policy prohibiting thousands of people, Jews and Gentiles alike, from leaving. The example of Sakharov proves it.

The *U. S. News & World Report* published in its June 18, 1973 issue an interview with Senator Jackson on the question of personal freedom in the Soviet Union, and on the question of whether the United States should be concerned about it. Senator Jackson said, "My interest here is to use our economic power to extend human freedom just a little bit. I think the greatest crime committeed by the Western world occurred during the 1930s, when we failed to listen to Winston Churchill. He alone cried out for action against Nazi Germany, and we stood idly by while millions of people were put in the ovens. We're on notice now that there are millions in Russia who want greater freedom. We know that many of them have been in concentration camps, and the things that are going on shock the conscience of people of good will everywhere. I'm disappointed with the President's position on all of this. I've been reading some statements that he made back in 1963. The United States, Richard Nixon said, should be willing to sell wheat to the satellite countries as a business deal provided that the government involved gives some greater degree of freedom to the people in these countries, in particular the freedom to emigrate. Well, I couldn't agree more. I'm just trying to implement his 1963 promise."

In the Soviet Union those who warn against strengthening the Russian military and the Russian economy by giving them our technological know-how and bailing them out whenever they have a crop failure, are branded as enemies of international peace. Actually the opposite is true. Those who believe that international politics should disregard the question of human freedom, that international treaties should be concluded regardless of the type of government the parties have, ignore the fact that a totalitarian society has no control over its rulers, and that by the very nature of totalitarianism, such a government feels insecure and wishes to extend its power in order to find more security which constantly eludes it. True peace can exist only when nations sincerely wish to live in peace with each other, and when freedom of the individual prevails everywhere, when mutual respect is more than just a slogan among nations, and when treaties are interpreted the same way and honored equally by all. Unfortunately, experts in semantical warfare know that this is not the case. Terms of international diplomacy may have two meanings, the normal one, and a special ideo-political twist given them by the Communists. Agreements may therefore be interpreted one way by the Western powers and another way by the Soviets. The Yalta and Potsdam agreements constitute eloquent proof of this fact. While the West kept to the language of these treaties and saw to it that the zones occupied by the Western powers united into a peaceful and democratic Germany, the Soviets prevented the unification of the zone under their control with the rest of the country and transformed it into a Communist state. The Soviets do intend the reunification of both German states, but on their terms. They want both to become Communist. The same tactics prevail in Korea.

North Korea speaks of reunification of both Koreas; that means for Pyongyang a united Communist Korea. In Vietnam the country was similarly divided into North and South; after five years of the most costly war and at a loss of more than fifty thousand lives the Americans concluded with the Communists an agreement that would divide South Vietnam into two zones, one Communist-dominated, the other under the control of Thieu. However, it is certain that such an agreement will not be honored and that Communists will never allow free elections in the zone under their control; on the contrary, they have been striving and will continue to strive to extend their domination over the entire Vietnam.

The euphoric "peaceful co-existence" in the name of which the Soviet Union now tries to obtain from the West the technology she has been unable to develop herself, has a Communist meaning too. In Russia there is the conviction that, in the long run, history is on the side of the Soviet Union. It is Brezhnev's and Kosygin's view that co-existence will have to be given a new turn whenever opportunities present themselves to obtain sudden and great advantages. This was already demonstrated in the recent crisis on the Middle East. History will be given a little nudge when there is the time to do so. In case we allow ourselves to be weakened, our economic and military power to be eclipsed by the Soviet Union, that nudge might become a shove.

Détente is desirable, but détente is not enough. For a lasting peace, freedom must reign everywhere. The people must be informed, made part of the decisions of their governments. Ideas and individuals must travel freely inside and across geographical borders. A utopian goal? Perhaps, but one that is made imperative by the atomic age when an abritrary government, a clique of madmen or a tyrant thirsty for power can initiate atomic warfare which would spell the destruction of mankind.

From a slogan, from a vision, universal freedom has become a condition sine qua non of mankind's survival.

Appendix I

THE JEWISH COUNCILS—
A CRUEL INVENTION

The Jewish Councils, called *Judenräte*, established by the Germans everywhere immediately after they occupied a country, constituted a satanic invention. Indeed they served to use the Jews as instruments for their own annihilation, as we shall see.

The Judenräte (plural of Judenrat) originated in 1939 in Poland, after that country succumbed to Hitler's Blitzkrieg.

On September 21st of that year, Heydrich Reinhard, chief of the SS Security Service, and assistant to Heinrich Himmler, chief of the SS (Storm Troopers, Hitler's Elite Army) sent the following instructions to the Corps commanders of his "Einsatzgruppen" (mobile troops):

> In each community a council of Jewish elders is to be set up. It is to be composed, as far as possible, of the remaining influential persons and rabbis. Depending on the size of the community, they should number up to twenty-four male members. This council is to be made fully responsible (in a literal sense of the word) for the exact and punctual implementation of all instructions released or yet to be released by us.

In keeping with these instructions, Judenräte were established throughout Hungary. It was enjoined to their members that they were to cooperate with the SS in order to avoid trouble for themselves as well as for their coreligionists. Thus, the members of these Jewish councils were put into a very special position, one which burdened them with tremendous responsibilities and aroused painful conflicts in their souls. The conflict imposed on them, namely whom to sacrifice first by designating him for deportation could be compared to the plight of a mother who would be asked which of her two sons she wished to save by sacrificing the other son. (A hypothesis which refers to an actual fact repeated during the Nazi era).

The reassurance given to the members of the Jewish Council to the effect that their fellow Jews would be spared any harm provided they obeyed the orders was a trick aimed at lulling the intended victims into security so that they may be deported to the extermination camps without giving any trouble to the authorities. Imagine the situation; hundreds of thousands of people living in terror, knowing that they are at the mercy of their worst enemies, fearing the worst. The enemies in question tell the leaders of these people that they have nothing to fear provided they obey their orders. The Jews, who had every reason to be pessimistic, are overjoyed; so it won't be as bad as they had feared, it will be possible to survive, to live with the new masters! They cling to this thin thread of hope, they will go out of their way to show their cooperation. . . . No trouble, no resistance is to be expected on their part whatever the demands of the Germans, whatever the measures taken by them may be.

How this deceit of the Jewish population through the intermediary of the Jewish Councils was carried out was demonstrated to me when the Judenrat was constituted in my native city of Kolozsvár. The report was spread in the ghetto that soon all inmates would be transported to camps in the "Motherland" (Hungary, as that country was called after World War I). There conditions would be better, all could be required to do only light labor.

Had the real facts, the real plans of the Nazis been known, many would have tried to escape to Rumania. Extreme desperation might even have prompted some to try armed resistance. All this was averted, thanks to the use of the Jewish Council. After all, prominent Jews, respected by the community, were telling their fellow Jews that no great harm would come to them, that by following orders they might even be spared the dangers and hardships of the war!

The members of the Jewish Council of Kolozsvár were to transmit orders communicated to them in such short intervals that it had hardly any time to assure their immediate execution. All places of worship and other buildings to be used by the German military were to be evacuated. All welfare funds collected by the Jewish organizations were to be handed over to the occupying power. All Jewish schools were to be closed. Jewish labor had to be made available upon immediate demand. These were the initial orders. Others followed shortly thereafter. Eventually all Jews were deported even faster than the Germans had originally planned, thanks to the overzealous efforts of their Hungarian accomplices, namely Undersecretaries Endre and Baky, the members of the Council along with the others.

Philip Freudiger, a former member of the Jewish Council in Budapest, escaped with his family to Rumania. I met him in Bucharest and he related to me the facts concerning the formation and operation of the Jewish Council in Budapest. On March 19, 1944, two German SS officers appeared at the offices of the Jewish community and requested an immediate meeting with officers of both Jewish congregations, the orthodox and modern sections. The meeting was hurriedly arranged. Freudiger was present at that meeting. It was attended by a certain Obersturmführer Krumey and Hauptsturmführer Wysliceni, and they were accompanied by two other SS officers. Obersturmführer

Krumey occupied the president's seat. Next to him was seated Wysliceni and one of the SS officers; the second officer was standing behind them with his gun pointed towards the officers of the congregations.

Following the identification of the Jewish participants, the presiding SS officer informed the representatives of the congregations that as of that moment all Jewish affairs would be administered by the SS and the SD (the German security force). Furthermore, Krumey informed the Jewish representatives that they would be individually and collectively responsible for the strict implementation of all instructions handed to them, and also that it would be their responsibility to maintain calm and order among the Jewish population. If they cooperated with the German authorities, no serious harm would occur to their coreligionists. A second meeting was ordered for the next day, to be attended by all the leaders of Jewish cultural institutions of the communities.

The cooperation on the German side was of a peculiar nature. On the twentieth and twenty-first of this month of March, 1944, a group of Jews were taken from their homes and transported to the Jewish theological seminary by the SS. There they were kept under constant surveillance. The names of the people arrested had been selected from a rather lengthy list. Who had supplied the SS with that list was never discovered. The men taken into custody ranged from physicians and businessmen to wealthy individuals, but also others who could by no means be considered as prominent men. They were to be hostages of the Germans for the strict, immediate and complete execution of their demands.

Freudiger then told me what happened further. Like in our own city of Kolozsvár the Germans strangled Jewish life by shutting off all Jewish institutions. They did so without attracting any attention, proceeding against each institution one by one. They closed down now a school, now a temple; then again ordered the evacuation of a hospital, a seminary. All Jewish property was confiscated. In this respect there seemed to be a rivalry between Germans and Hungarians. As we have related in a previous chapter, the Hungarian government also ordered the confiscation of all Jewish assets and incomes from whatever source they might have come. In addition, the German secret police was constantly on the alert, ready to arrest Jews at random. As a result the pulse of daily life came to a quick stop in the Jewish community. Synagogues were no longer visited since worshippers were arrested on the spot and deported to the concentration camp of Kistarcsa. Jews did not dare to communicate with each other. They remained hidden in their apartments, living in complete solitude. Their telephones were cut off by decree of the government. They did not dare to show themselves on the streets. In fact, Eichmann made it his favorite sport to arrest Jews and deport them for the sole purpose of striking terror into Jewish hearts.

In Hungary the liquidation of the Jewish population proceeded faster than elsewhere in Europe. We have already told the reason for this. Undersecretary Endre, in charge of Jewish Affairs, was racing against time. He realized that the Germans had lost the war and knew that public opinion would soon turn against the occupants. He wished to finish with the Jewish question before the Allies had finished with the Germans and their Hungarian accomplices. It seems now, from a historical perspective, that the fate of more than eight hundred thousand Hungarian Jews had been decided because of a sort of personal vendetta of one rabid anti-semite. This could happen, as we have pointed out, because of the inertia and the indifference of the outside world. As to the Hungarian Judenräte, no other Jewish organization anywhere was exposed to so much criticism after the war. This went so far as to accusing them of cooperation with the Nazis in the systematic extermination of the Jewish population of Hungary. A number of books have been published that are concerned with the tragedy of Hungarian Jewry. The best known of them are Reitlinger's *The Final Solution*,* and Raoul Hilberg's *The Destruction of European Jews*.** Both treat the question of the responsibility of the Hungarian Judenräte in a one-sided way, presenting only the charges against the latter without taking into account the extenuating circumstances in their defense. The reason for this is that at the time of the publication of these books, the authors could rely only on source materials that were based on data either unproven or insufficiently proven. After World War II the archives that could have established the truth about the events were not yet open to historians. Now, however, Dr. Randolph L. Braham, professor at the City University of New York, jointly with the World Federation of Hungarian Jews, is making serious efforts to write objective history with reference to the role of the Hungarian Jewish Councils and to the tragedy of Hungarian Jews in general. Recently the third volume of Hungarian Jewish Studies was published under the editorship of Professor Braham. It presents for the first time the statements made by members of the councils, along with a description of the circumstances under which they operated. The publication of the statements of the former members of the councils and that of the charges levelled against them will have to be weighed against each other. The fact seems to emerge from the reading of this third volume of Jewish studies that the council members undoubtedly committed many mistakes, and that their judgment had not always been the best. This does not mean that they were guilty of collaboration with the Nazis. One also has to take into account the fact that the deportation of the Jews of Hungary was accomplished in great haste and that no one, not even people close to the occupants or to the circles of the Hungarian government knew exactly what was planned from one day to the other.

---

*Reitlinger: *The Final Solution*, (New York, Random House, 1968).
**Raoul Hilberg: *The Destruction of the Hungarian Jews*, (Chicago, Quadrangle Books, 1967).

Dr. Rudolf Kastner, about whose role in the negotiations with Eichmann we have already spoken, summarized the activities of the Judenräte in Hungary as follows, "The process by which the members of the Councils became gradually more and more submissive to the Nazis can be ascribed to the systematic and deceptive methods employed by the Nazis. Step by step they were made tractable. In the beginning relatively unimportant things were asked of them; replacable things of material value like possessions, money and apartments. Later, however, the personal freedom of the human being was demanded. Finally, the Nazis asked for life itself. This gradualism in demands, coupled with ever increasing terror, was an ingenious and effective phychological device."*

Though the plan of extermination of the Jews was the same throughout Europe, the methods employed to this end varied. The relying on the Judenrat as a convenient intermediary for the organization of the deportations was general, but then again the scope of their operations, the time allotted to them, the means at their disposal to help their coreligionists were different. In Western Europe the Judenrat was in charge of the administration of the ghettos. In Poland, at the beginning of the occupation of that country by the Nazis, the Jewish Council had a certain latitude to help the inmates of the ghettos.

The survivors of the Wlodowa Ghetto in Poland revealed the following facts. The Jewish Council selected from the ghetto people to be transported to an unspecified location for work. As these people never came back, the suspicion that they were murdered arose soon.

Rabbi Leiner, the well-known rabbi of Radzyn, had a talk with the members of the Jewish Council and said to them, "Why don't you tell the people the truth? If they knew it, some may decide to resist: some may attempt to run away to a nearby forest; no matter what chances they

---

*See *Encyclopedia Judaica*, Volume 8, pp. 883ff.

might take, they would know what is awaiting them."

However, the members of the Jewish Council were under terrible pressure by the Gestapo to keep silent as to the ultimate destination of the people they sent away. Thereupon, Rabbi Leiner himself went among the people and told them the truth. This caused great agitation and unrest among the inhabitants of the ghetto. The SS became aware of the fact that the rabbi was arousing the people. They decided to make an example of his punishment.

One day in June, 1942, the SS called together the people of the ghetto and led them to the marketplace in the city. There, in front of all those assembled, young and old, Rabbi Leiner was hanged. His last words were the beginning of the ancient Jewish prayer, "Shema Yisroel Adonoy Eloyhenoo Adonoy Echod," "Hear, O Israel, the Lord is Our God, the Lord is One." The public at the feet of the gallows had to attend the convulsions and final agony of the holy man, after which they were returned to the ghetto. A few of them succeeded subsequently in fleeing to Warsaw and some joined partisan groups. Of course, the immense majority of the ghetto people were annihilated, including the members of the Jewish Council.

In retrospect, one is disinclined to condemn the council members in the ghettos of Hungary or elsewhere for not being sincere with their fellow Jews. They lived under superhuman pressure. Whatever they did, someone would have to be sacrificed. The conflicts and dramas in the souls of these men were extraordinarily intense. It is understandable that most of them thought that by obeying the Germans, their own lives would be spared. Who would have the greatness to rise above such a thought in their situation? Also, one must take into account that by disobeying the Germans they risked entailing horrible retaliation against the very same people they tried to protect. The example of Rabbi Leiner is conclusive in this respect. It is known that they were torn apart by contradictory forces, incapable of standing the mental torture. They were suffering great mental anguish which caused a number of the members of the various Jewish Councils to commit suicide.

The concept and organization of the Judenräte were, as we have pointed out in the beginning of this chapter, a diabolical invention, worthy of the German Nazis.

Appendix II

A SHORT HISTORY OF HUNGARIAN ANTI-SEMITISM—THE ACCUSATION OF RITUAL MURDER OF TISZA ESZLÁR

In 1867 the Hungarian nation, that had fought for its independence against the Habsburg dynasty, made an agreement with the latter. In the terms of this agreement, all nationalities were to be considered equal within the Austro-Hungarian Federation, and by the same token, the agreement confirmed the freedom of religion, proclaimed by the Hungarian revolution of 1848.

Under the long reign of Emperor Franz Joseph (King Ferenc József, as the Hungarians called him) which lasted until the end of World War I in 1918, the situation of the Hungarian Jews was, in general, favorable. Officially no obstacles were put in the way of their advancement in the careers or in the economic life of the country, though in fact, there remained a deep-rooted social prejudice against them which made their assimilation with the rest of the nation difficult if not impossible. A few Jews, especially if converted, succeeded in attaining high positions in the army. Jewish tycoons of industry obtained Hungarian nobility, acquired the title of "Baron" though never that of "Count," which was reserved to descendants of the ancient feudal families. There were even a few who were appointed "Royal Counsellors," a largely honorary title which however carried great prestige with it.

As a result of the liberal policies of the monarchy, Jews made great strides in the professions, stimulated the economy and the cultural life of the nation. They became the yeast that made the rich intellectual substance of the nation ferment with the addition of new ideas. They actually formed a link to the Western world.

In spite of all the above, anti-semitism began to raise its ugly head in Hungarian politics and in the life of the nation in the 1880s, hardly a decade after the national reconciliation with Austria. A new political movement, headed by Gyula Verhovay, a member of the Chamber of Deputies, inscribed it on its flag. It was the only program of Verhovay's party. His followers founded newspapers, clubs, fraternities, sent out speakers to the four corners of the country spreading the doctrine that the Jews were an alien body in the nation, with ideals pernicious to the moral health of Hungarians. Verhovay's influence was widespread among the people. Its penetration was demonstrated by what was called the Hungarian Dreyfus Affair that had its repercussion throughout the entire European continent.

On the first of April, 1882, a young servant girl by the name of Esther Solymossi was sent by her mistress to fetch some housepaint from a store in the old part of the village Tisza Eszlár, a small commuity on the Tisza river. The girl left early in the morning and did not return. As the time of the year was that of the Jewish Passover, the rumor spread that the Jews had killed her to mix her blood into their unleavened bread, an old abject accusation that had been used throughout the centuries to justify atrocities against the Jews. It was revived in Tisza Eszlár and officially adopted by the local authorities. The latter based their investigation of the disappearance of Esther on this myth. They interrogated all Jewish families in the locality. By threats and promises they induced Moritz Scharf, the 8-year-old son of the ritual Jewish butcher, to testify to the effect that he had seen his father, aided by others, take little Esther to the synagogue, cut her throat and pour her blood into a basin.

The testimony of the little boy was of course insufficient

in law, and more evidence was needed to prove the charge. It would have been necessary to find the body of the girl with her throat slit open. The body however, remained undiscoverable, till one day the river washed ashore a body that was recognized by most of those who had known her as that of the missing girl, even though her features had been made unrecognizable because of the body's long stay in the water. The body bore no trace of violence of any sort. The overzealous magisrates of the village and of the nearby town Nyiregyháza, refused to accept the testimony of the witnesses. They kept all the Jews of the village in jail and arrested others, surveyors of lumber rafts on the river, on a charge of complicity. They maintained that the lumbermen had smuggled the body ashore in order to create an alibi for their coreligionaries of Tisza Eszlár. However, the time passed and no other body could be discovered which resembled even vaguely the body of Esther Solymossy.

The Tisza Eszlár ritual murder charge, or the Affair, as it was briefly called, alarmed the entire Jewish population of Hungary. They hired a liberal and respected lawyer, Károly Eötvös, to come to the rescue of the defendants. Eötvös started an investigation of his own—impeded whenever possible by the local authorities—and established the fact that the little girl had been systematically mistreated and half-starved by her mistress. Suicide because of despondency was the only plausible explanation of her death.

The trial took place in 1883 in Budapest. It was attended by the representatives not only of the national press, but also by those of many Western countries and even of the United States. It ended by the acquittal of the defendants. The acquittal did not heal however the moral wounds caused by the Affair. Suspicion against the Jews persisted in the hearts of many Hungarians who believed and were told that the Jews had bribed the judges to save themselves. It took some time before the waves of distrust and hatred subsided somewhat.

The end of the 19th century brought a relative calm in the relationship between Jews and non-Jews in Hungary.

During the First World War Jewish families suffered their share of losses of their members on the battlefields, and their heartaches and worries concerning their beloved ones. There was hardly any Jewish family that did not have one or several of them killed, crippled or taken prisoner. In spite of that, malicious persons spread the slander that the Jews had been able to keep out of the war, and that they had enriched themselves as suppliers of the armies. Inevitably some Jewish financiers profited from the scarcity of materials and from large benefits from contracts they obtained from the armies, but the same was true of non-Jewish industrialists. The greatest scandal concerning reckless profiteering from military orders was connected with the name of Archduke Frederick, who had supplied boots with paper soles that were given to soldiers in the cold winter on Russian and other battlefields. The feet of thousand of these unfortunates were frozen and had to be amputated.

The First World War ended as it is well known, by the defeat of Hungary and her allies. The front disintegrated, the soldiers flocked home in groups or individually. The end of the war saw the formation of a new anti-semitic movement called the Awakening Hungarians. Its members were recruited from among the disgruntled elements of the lower middle classes, from non-commissioned officers, small clerks with a sprinkling of a few officers. Later the movement was taken over by politicians close to Nicholas Horthy, the future regent of Hungary.*

After the Hungarian revolution of 1938 the Republic was proclaimed. Count Michael Károlyi, a liberal politician

---

*After the advent of Nicholas Horthy, Tibor Eckhardt, who had headed the Section of Foreign Affairs in Horthy's exiled government in Siófok, and was the head of the Department of Press of the Regent from 1920 to 1922, became the president of the Association of the Awakening Hungarians in 1923.

and head of the Parliamentary opposition of the government during the war years, was elected its first president. He was an avowed friend of the Western allies. With the dissolution of the fronts, the disorderly retreat of the armies, and especially as a result of the occupation of Hungarian territories by Rumanian, Czech and Yugoslav troops, each of which wished to create accomplished facts in anticipation of the peace treaties, the economic and political situation inside of what remained of Hungary became more and more difficult, its administration more and more chaotic. The time was ripe for Hungarian Communist agitators, many of whom had been sitting out the war in Moscow, to return home and begin their propaganda. The new government of the mutilated country at first jailed a number of them, but was discouraged by fruitless negotiations with the victorious Allies in regard to the withdrawal of foreign troops, and the opening of supply routes for Hungary. Also, because of internal dissension among its members, it threw in the sponge, released the Communist leaders from jail and handed the power over to them. Thus, the first Hungarian Soviet Republic was born. It called itself the Revolutionary Committee of Workers and Soldiers. Its president was Sándor Garbai, a non-Jewish Social Democrat, but the strong man in the new government was Béla Kun, Moscow-trained, and a personal friend of Lenin. Béla Kun was Jewish and so were two or three other members of his regime. This fact was sufficient for many to equate Communism with the Jews and to declare that the Jews were out to rule the world, and that all Jews were enemies of the nation and the enemies of mankind. This was the same yarn spun later by the Nazis. The accusation of the desire for world domination by Jews originated in the Western world and in our time in Hungary.

The regime of Béla Kun lasted exactly 100 days, from March 20 to August 1, 1919. On that latter day the Communist leaders fled to Vienna. They were succeeded by a provisional government of Social-Democrats. The designation of the Hungarian form of government was changed from "Hungarian Soviet Republic" to "Democratic Republic of Hungary." The first act of the new cabinet was to give amnesty to all persons arrested by the Communists for counter-revolutionary activities.

The resignation and fall of the Communist government was due to the defeat of the Red Army on the former borders of the country, the encirclement of the capital by foreign troops, and to the widespread hunger and discontent prevailing among the population. On the other side of the Danube river at Szeged, a White Army composed of former army officers and soldiers recruited by them, was waiting. Upon the news of the collapse of the Béla Kun regime, this army supported by French, Czech and Rumanian troops, crossed the Danube and entered western Hungary. The counter-revolution was triumphant. Its advent was marked by the systematic persecution of and hideous excesses committed against the Jews.

The counter-revolution was headed by Nicholas Horthy, a former admiral in the navy of the Austro-Hungarian monarchy. Sitting on a white horse, Horthy entered the capital to be proclaimed Regent.

Officers among those closest to Horthy, notably his nephew Ivan Héjjas, Gyula Gömbös and many others operating through individual groups called "detachments" ferreted out Jews, especially well-to-do Jews, in the cities. They accused them of complicity with the Communists although most of their men were by the very nature of their economic situation, hostile to Communism. These Jews were dragged from their homes and taken to the cellars of hotels where the officers had established their headquarters, and beaten mercilessly. They were usually released after payment of very large sums, often their entire fortune. The list of the victims grew very long. One of those who died of his wounds in the first days of the operations of the Horthy detachments was Ignace Harsai, owner of a picture gallery. Another was Isidor Neubauer, owner of a match

factory. Poor people such as Ferenc Fodor, a mechanic, Jenö Wertheimer, a 17-year-old student, also succumbed needlessly to the furor of purification of these officers.*
The most notorious among the Jew beaters and torturers next to Héjjas were Pál Pronay and Michael Francia Kis, a sadist, who many years later was arrested as a mass murderer. They soon realized that there was money to be made from the terrorizing of the Jews. They levied a special tax on the wealthy ones. Héjjas later became a member of the Hungarian Parliament and was openly accused by a fellow deputy of repeatedly taking "loans" from a Jew named Lederer.*
In the provinces the anti-Jewish terror, cloaked under the label of anti-Communism, raged even more fiercely than in Budapest. Special camps were established at different places, camps of torture, and of inhuman mistreatment. Camps that became in Hungary as notorious as have become the names of Auschwitz, Dachau, Treblinka and other infamous camps of Hitler.
Regent Horthy, to whom protests were made by politicians about the excesses committed by his officers, officially condemned these excesses but did nothing to suppress them. To quiet public opinion at home and abroad, he ordered an investigation. The fact was established that many of the officers' victims were murdered and robbed. In spite of this, the investigating authorities did not recommend the prosecution of the criminals. On November 3, 1921, Horthy issued an order of amnesty on behalf of those who "committed certain excesses not for the sake of self-enrichment but under the influence of public exasperation against the perpetrators of acts undermining the interests of the Hungarian fatherland and the Hungarian race" during the revolutions between the 31st of October, 1918 and

---
*See Elek Karsai, *A budai Sándor Palotában Történt.* (It happened in the Sándor Palace of Buda), a chronicle of the events in Budapest from 1919-1941 (Budapest, 1964), p. 32.
*Ibid., p. 55.

the 20th of March, 1920, that is, between the periods of the Károlyi and the Communist revolutions. Héjjas thus could continue to murder and rob his victims and was rewarded for these patriotic acts by his election to the House of Representatives in 1926.

The Minister of the Interior serving under Horthy, Ödön Beniczky, worried about the anti-Jewish excesses, bluntly asked the Regent, "Will there be any progroms in Hungary?"

Horthy answered, "There will be no progroms but a few will take a bath" (meaning, will be drowned in the Danube).**

One of the first men "to take a bath" was Béla Somogyi, the Jewish editor-in-chief of the workers' newspaper *Népszava*. His body was floating in the river on February 10, 1920.

The terror against the Jews was concomitant with measures of terror taken against the entire population. The terror was to cover up the fact that the new rulers did nothing to alleviate the deep misery of the people. The Jews were once again made the scapegoats for all the woes that beset the masses.

The stamp was put on the official character of the anti-semitism of the new regime by the restrictions on the admission of Jewish students to national universities. In the summer of 1920 the Hungarian Minister of Education issued an ordinance "to limit the number of students admissible to national universities on the basis of their nationality or race." This ordinance was uniquely and specifically aimed at the Jews. No restrictions were imposed upon the admission of students of other minorities. Only 6% of Jewish applicants were to be admitted. The edict gave no specifics as to the criteria for admission, nor was any exception made in favor of those Jewish students who had fought and distinguished themselves during the war. They as well

---

**Ibid., p. 25.

as their other coreligionists were barred from pursuing their studies in the country for which they had shed their blood. As one Hungarian poet put it, "I looked around and found not my home in my homeland."

The very few Jewish students who succeeded in being admitted had to endure all kinds of humiliations. They were frequently beaten up by their fellow students without any protection on the part of the university authorities, let alone of the police. At the University of Budapest they had to sit in the last benches of the classrooms called "benches of shame." They were made to feel that it was shameful and degrading to belong to the Jewish race.

The "numerus clausus" as the ordinance in question was named, constituted the first act of official anti-semitism in Europe in modern times. Under Horthy, Hungary became the forerunner of Jewish persecution as a means of political propaganda, a movement that was instrumental in the unleashing of World War II. One can state without exaggeration that the racist policy adopted by Horthy and his government created a new era of backwardness and prejudice against minorities that had been banned from the European continent since the end of the 19th century. In only one respect did the Hungarian "numerus clausus" benefit other nations—Jewish students who could not resign themselves to being indefinitely cut off from knowledge and learning emigrated en masse. Many were poor as church mice and had to struggle against the greatest odds, but a great number of them became prominent scholars, scientists, and professionals in the countries of their adoption, enriching the intellectual life of the latter. In every major country of the world, including the United States, Jewish scholars of Hungarian birth contributed to the development of knowledge as teachers, writers or researchers.

The activities of the officers' detachments did not abate in spite of official and rather lukewarm disavowal. The people came to hate them and call them "bandits with crane feathers," from the feathers they wore stuck in their caps. On July 20, 1920, one of these illegal groups, its members armed with revolvers and bayonets, attacked the guests at the Café Club, a fashionable private club in the section of the capital called Lipótváros, a residential neighborhood chiefly inhabited by Jewish businessmen and industrialists. Two of the guests were killed, ten were gravely wounded, and others escaped with light injuries. The attack was planned, as was proved later on, by the Awakening Hungarians, the association presided over by the Regents' nephew. The police, of course, failed to intervene. The affair stirred up enough emotion to cause Joseph Bottlik, vice-president of the Natonal Assembly to bring up the subject in Parliament. He deplored it and declared that "this could happen only because similar attacks had remained unpunished in the past."

The "numerus clausus" was not the only manifestation of anti-semitism that made Hungary the forerunner of Hitlerism. Concurrently with its publication, enthusiastic propagandists advocated theories later adopted by Hitler. Horthy himself urged in the cabinet meeting of March 18, 1933, presided over by him, that Hungary should enact "laws for the protection of the race." Perhaps his attitude was influenced by a memorandum he had received from a physician by the name of Ferenc Tömösváry, the authorship of which Hitler would have gladly accepted. This memorandum sent to Horthy was the transcript of an article by the same writer, rejected by all scientific publications in Hungary. Tömösváry started with the premise that "the lower classes have a much higher birthrate than the upper strata of society and urged the prevention of the multiplication of such classes detrimental to the purity of the race." In plain English, Tömösváry advocated already at that time, the sterilization of the weak. He concluded, "A powerful central authority that will disregard the often false and hypocritic sentimentalism of our era, conscious of its responsibility toward the race, will perhaps accomplish such a step, but not societies based on democracy and parliamentarism."*

Several Hungarian politicians such as László Endre, the future secretary of state, a sworn enemy of the Jews, Gyula Gömbös, Horthy's friend who became prime minister in 1932, and others started a movement to steer Hungarian foreign policy in the direction of a close association with Adolf Hitler. Gömbös himself paid a visit to Hitler as early as 1920, when Hitler was still nothing but the leader of a noisy and obnoxious political movement. After his advent on June 20, 1933, to the prime ministry, Gömbös declared that "Hitler is here to stay and so is fascism." He saluted Hitler after his elevation to the federal chancellorship and declared that he was proud of being his friend. It was this orientation of the Hungarian authorities toward Germany that made the occupation of the country and the deportation of Hungarian Jews such an easy task for the Nazis in the last phase of World War II.

The increasing influence of Germany on Hungarian national politics, especially the attitude of the Hungarian government toward the Jews, is evidenced by the anti-Jewish laws that followed the "numerus clausus." The law of November 20, 1920, ordered the explusion from Hungary of all Jews who had immigrated to the country after 1914. This law was promulgated at a time when there were pressing questions to settle, such as the resettlement of refugees from former Hungarian territories. The easy solution that presented itself to the lawmakers was to expell the Jews, and settle the refugees in their place. However, the number of the possible expellees was too "insignificant" to cope with the problem.

The law of 1920 was superseded by that of 1925. Paragraph 15 of the latter, point 7, declared that any foreigner who had entered the country as a result of an

---

*See the documentary *Horthy Miklós Titkos Iratai* (The Secret archives of Nicholas Horthy), by Kossuth Könyvkiadó (Budapest, 1963), p. 136.

immigration movement contrary to the interest of the state must be expelled, and his return should be forbidden. As one can see, the law was vaguely worded and allowed any interpretation. The then Minister of the Interior Gyula Kallay declared that this law of 1925 actually fostered the interests of the native Jewish population. He probably meant that it was the immigration of foreign Jews who caused rising anti-semitism from which all Jews, regardless of their origin, suffered, but such a contention, if that was the meaning of the statement of the prime minister, did not stand up in the light of the previous attacks on Jews, as I have related in the preceding pages.

In keeping with the spirit of the law of 1925, the Minister of the Interior sent special instructions to local authorities enjoining them to apply the strictest measures to prevent a "Jewish invasion." At the same time, Hungarian industries and commercial enterprises were instructed to review the necessity to employ foreign (meaning Jewish) workers, and asked them to get rid of the latter as soon as possible. The circular of the Minister pointed out that many Hungarians had emigrated because of the lack of opportunities at home while the Jewish population was increasing.*

In compliance with the appeal of the Minister many raids were staged in that year of 1925 against Jewish families and enterprises. As a result of these raids, the official statistics mentioned that 160 Jews with 183 members of their families were expelled immediately. Expulsion proceedings were started in 354 additional cases involving 824 Jewish persons, and 1383 heads of Jewish families with 3113 members were summoned to prove their right to stay in Hungary.

The law of 1925 itself was invalidated by that of 1938, Article XV, called "the law to assure a better balance in Hungarian social and economic life," a strange and telling title. This law limited the proportion of Jews admissible

---

*Ibid., pp. 87-88.

to the professions of journalism, filmmaking, of the stage, as well as to membership in the Bar Association and in the medical profession to 20%. Any industrial enterprise employing more than 10 workers was also limited to 20% of Jewish employment.

One year later, Article IV of the law of 1939 bore even more clearly the imprint of the Rassentheorie of Rosenberg and Hitler. It defined an answer to the question—who is considered to be a Jew? Any person either of Jewish faith or having one parent or two grandparents of that faith was classified in that category. Jews were barred from employment in the civil service (they had been de facto long before). The profession of a teacher at any level was forbidden to them. The numerus clausus, that is to say, the limitation of Jewish students in Hungarian universities was reaffirmed. Their proportion remained the same—6%. The same percentage was applied to licences in any trade. The law also curtailed the right to vote of Jews in Hungary.

The third and last Jewish law promulgated by the government under the regency of Nicholas Horthy was the Law of 1941, Article XV. This one was entitled, "Law for the supplementation and modification of the law of 1894," relative to the right to contract marriage, also the "Law" regarding the protection of the race deriving from the aforesaid law (of 1894). The gist of this last law was that the right to marry a non-Jew was denied to a Jewish person.

The anti-semitic laws in Hungary in their increasingly hostile attitude toward the Jewish populations reflect the gradual transformation of the Hungarian state from a feudal form of government that secured a relative freedom of the individuals within the limit of their respective spheres into a totalitarian state, a model for the German Nazis. These laws laid the foundations for the subsequent despoliation of the Jews, the deprivation of their rights as citizens and human beings. They actually delivered the Jews of Hungary who survived the cruel deportations to the native Arrow-Crossists. The latter openly aimed at their annihilation from which they were prevented only by the arrival of the Russian troops in Budapest.

In summary, one can state that official anti-semitism, that is to say, anti-semitism legally adopted as national and governmental policy, originated in modern times in Hungary. The leaders of that country, under the regency of Nicholas Horthy, can be regarded as teachers of the German Nazis.

Because of this fact, Hungary's role in spite of her small size, was very important in the history of the twentieth century.

The actual collaboration of the Hungarian leaders with the German National-Socialists constituted the framework within which unfolded the personal life story of the author.

INDEX OF PERSONS

ALDRIN, Edwin E., *134*
AMALRIK, Andrei, *165*
ANTONESCU, Ion, *64, 109*

BAKY, Laszlo, *15, 16, 26, 37, 52, 80, 81, 125, 175*
BELDING, Don, *122*
BENCZE, Minister of the Interior, *82*
BENICZKY, Odon, *82, 190*
BERNADOTTE, Count Folke, *105, 108, 109*
BOTTLIK, Joseph, *192*
BRAHAM, Randolph L., *178*
BRAND, Joel, *47, 48, 49, 51, 52, 53, 55, 56, 87, 88, 89*
BREZHNEV, Leonid, *159, 161, 162, 171*
BUBER, Martin, *156*

CAMPBELL, Sam, *122*
CECIL, George W., *156*
CHURCHILL, Sir Winston, *66, 129, 130, 148, 169*
COLLINS, Albert, *122*
CRANBORNE, British Colonial Secretary, *141*

DIRKSEN, Senator Everett, *117*
DOSTOEVSKI, Fedor Mikhailovich, *135, 136*
DREYFUS, Alfred, *15*
DUBCHECK, Alexander, *159*
DUCA, Gheorge Ion, *101*

EBAN, Aba, *145*
EHRENBURG, Ilya, *152*
EHRENPREIS, Marcus, *101*
EICHMANN, Adolf, *48, 50, 51, 52, 53, 56, 57, 80, 81, 82, 87, 88, 89, 95, 142, 177, 179*
EINSTEIN, Albert, *133*
EISENHOWER, Dwight D., *55*
ELDERS OF ZION, *16*

ENDRE, Laszlo, 15, 16, 24, 26, 37, 52, 54, 80, 81, 127, 175, 177, 193
EOTVOS, Karoly, 185
ESZLAR, Tisza, 15, 184, 185

FERENCI, Colonel, 82
FISCHER, Keresztes, 8
FODOR, Ferenc, 189
FRANASOVICI, Ambassador, 95, 99
FRANKL, Victor, 137
FRAWLEY, Patrick J., 123
FREUDIGER, Phillip, 48, 49, 51, 57, 175

GAFENCU, Grigore, 110
GAGARIN, Yuri, 134
GANDHI, Karamchand, 129
GARBAI, Sandor, 187
GOETHE, Von Johann, 133
GOMBOS, Gyula, 188, 193
GROMYKO, A. Andrei, 85
GROSZ, Bandi, 53

HALBERTSTAM, SHOLOM Eliezer, 127
HARRIMAN, Averell, 89
HARSAI, Ignace, 188
HEJJAS, Ivan, 188, 189, 190
HILBERG, Raoul, 178
HIMMLER, Heinrich, 173
HIRSCHMAN, Ira, 88, 89
HITLER, Adolf, x, etc.
HOCHHUTH, Rolf, 146
HORTHY, Nicholas (Miklos), 6, 11, 12, 82, 83, 186, 188, 189, 190, 191, 192, 195, 196
HUXLEY, Aldous, 113, 119, 135

IBSEN, Henrik, 97

JACKSON, Senator Henry, 168, 169
JAROSS, Andor, 15
JEFFERSON, President Thomas, 131
JOHNSON, James E., 122
JOSEPH, Franz, 183

KALLAY, Gyula, *186, 194*
KAROLYI, Count Michael, *12, 189*
KASTNER, Rudolf, *45, 47, 48, 49, 51, 52, 53, 56, 57, 101, 179*
KENNEDY, President John F., *158, 162*
KERSEY, Vierling, *123*
KIROV, Sergei, *167*
KIS, Michael Francia, *189*
KNIGHT, Goodwin, *119*
KOSYGIN, Aleksei, *159, 171*
KRASIN, Victor, *166*
KRUMEY, Herman, *48, 50, 175, 176*
KRUSHCHEV, Nikita, *152, 158, 159, 161, 162, 164*
KULIKOV, General V., *162*
KUN, Andras, *83, 85*
KUN, Bela, *12, 187, 188*
KUZNETSOV, Anatoli, *150, 151, 152*

LAZAR, General, *80*
LEINER, Samuel Solomon, *179, 180*
LENIN, Vladimir Ilyich, *150, 159, 167, 187*
LEWENSTEIN, Daniel, *63*
LINCOLN, President Abraham, *130, 137*
LOEBEL, Evzen, *67*

McCAIN, John S., *126*
McCOMB, Marshall F., *122, 123*
MALINOVSKY, Marshall, *85*
MASARYK, Jan, *105*
MASARYK, Thomas, *105*
MENGELE, Josef, *103*
MICHAEL, King of Rumania, *64, 109, 110*
MORGENTHAU, Henry, *144*

NAGY, Imre, *158*
NEUBAUER, Isidor, *188*
NIEMOLLER, Martin, *x*
NIXON, President Richard M., *169*

PATTON, General George Smith, *94*
PAUKER, Anna, *67, 109, 110*
PAULUS, Friedrich, *150*

PIUS XII, Pope, *80 146*
PODGORNY, Nicholai, *152*
POLIAKOV, Leon, *146*
POP, Jonel, *5, 9, 16, 18*
PRONAY, Pal, *189*
PUSHKIN, Aleksandr, *168*
PUTNAM, George, *123*

RADESCU, Nicolae, *66, 72, 110*
REINHARD, Heidrich, *173*
RONCALLI, Monsignor Angelo, *81*
ROOSEVELT, President Franklin Delano, *25, 26, 66, 80, 88, 130, 131, 143, 144*
ROSENBERG, Alfred, *16*
ROTTA, Monsignor Angelo, *84*
ROUSSEAU, Jean Jacques, *167*

SAKHAROV, Andrei, *162, 163, 164, 165, 166, 168,* 69
SAKHAROV, Andrei, 62, *163, 164, 165, 166, 168. 169*
SCHARF, Moritz, *184*
SCHMIDT, Reichswehr Officer, *47, 48, 49, 50*
SCHOPENHAUER, Arthur, *68*
SENECA, Annaeus, *68*
SHAW, George Bernard, *x*
SHELL, Joe, *119*
SHERTOK, Moshe, *88*
SLANSKY, Rudolf, *67*
SOLYMOSSI, Esther, *15, 184, 185*
SOMOGYI, Bela, *190*
SOLZHENITSYN, Alexander, *150, 164, 165, 167, 168*
SPIEGEL, Bernard, *122*
STALIN, Joseph, *87, 109, 148, 149, 150, 152, 155, 159, 164*
STEINHARDT, Ambassador, *87*
SZALASI, Ferenc, *83, 84*
SZTOJAY, Dome, *9, 15*

TATARESCU, George, *64, 65, 105*
THOMPSON, R. S., *122*
TOMOSVARY, Ferenc, *192*
TOYNBEE, Arnold, *123, 158*
TROTSKY, Lev Davidovich, *150*

TRUMAN, President Harry, *109*
VERHOVAY, Gyula, *11, 184*
VISHINSKY, Andrei, *69, 70, 72, 76*
VISHOIANU, Foreign Minister, *110*
VOLPE, John A., *123*
VON ZELL, Harry, *122*

WALLENBERG, Raoul, *78, 82, 83, 84, 85, 86, 102, 105*
WASHINGTON, President George, *131*
WEISS, Joseph, *127*
WELK, Lawrence, *123*
WERTHEIMER, Jeno, *189*
WINNIGER, Joseph, *47, 48, 50*
WISE, Stephen, *143, 144*
WISLICENI, Dieter, *48, 49, 50, 175, 176*
WURMBRAND, Richard, *x*

YAKIR, Pyotr, *167*
YEVTUSHENKO, Yevgeni Alexandrovich, *150*

ZAKHAROV, V. Marshall, *162*